Baby Signs

The Zodiac guide to your little star

SARAH BARTLETT

A GODSFIELD BOOK
www.godsfieldpress.com

First published in Great Britain in 2005
by Godsfield Press, a division of
Octopus Publishing Group Ltd
2–4 Heron Quays
Docklands, London E14 4JP

10 9 8 7 6 5 4 3 2 1

Printed and bound in China

ISBN 1 84181 282 X
EAN 9781841812823

A CIP catalogue record for this book is
available from the British Library

Disclaimer
This book is intended to give general
information only. The publisher, author
and distributor expressly disclaim all
liability to any person arising directly or
indirectly from the use of, or any errors or
omissions in, the information in this book.
The adoption and application of the
information in this book is at the reader's
discretion and is their sole responsibility.

Contents

Twinkle, twinkle little star, how I wonder what you are!

This book is a fun, insightful zodiac guide to good parenting for newborns to 24 months. Not only will you understand how your baby ticks, but you'll also discover how to help develop the little angel's gifts and talents so that he or she grows into a unique, loving child.

Why astrology?

Astrology is widely accepted as a valuable psychological tool that can be used to increase our understanding of others. Bringing a baby into the world is a big responsibility and, as for any new journey, we need some kind of map in order to find the best route to take. Sun-sign astrology is non-judgemental and can help you nurture your baby's qualities, giving him or her the best possible start in life.

Born on the cusp?

Being born 'on the cusp' means being born on the day that the sun moves from one zodiac sign into another. Someone might say 'Oh, I was born on the cusp, I'm bit Aries and a bit Taurus, that's why I'm so confused!' but this isn't true. The sun changes signs at different times of the day depending on the year, and sometimes the actual day changes too. So if your baby is born 'on the cusp', you need to check which sun sign he or she really is. You can contact me on my website to find out for free (see below). Then you can say to your baby 'You're a Taurus not an Aries!' End of confusion.

The right kind of love

Babies want to please their parents as much as parents want to please their babies. But, as parents, we can unintentionally try to make our babies into people they're not. We unconsciously expect our children to behave according to our own personal likes and dislikes – and that's when we clash! Depending on his or her sun-sign personality, your baby will thrive on different kinds of nurturing. Know the right way to love him or her and you will be rewarded with a happy baby.

SARAH BARTLETT
www.sarahbartlett.com

Aries

MARCH 21 TO APRIL 19

Before you know it, I'll be talking, walking and giving you the biggest hugs you can imagine. Bold and brave, I'm passionate about life and people.

Look at me!

Right from the word go, baby Aries is ready for adventure, excitement, mischief and exploration. He'll demand to be fed at the most unpredictable times and will scream out loud in the small hours just to generate excitement. This little soul simply wants to be the boss and to do what he wants, when it suits him. Sounds like a challenge? It needn't be, if you keep one step ahead of this feisty little character. Show your eager go-getter something new each day, and praise him for being the pioneering person he's destined to become.

Aries babies thrive on fantasy, daring and provocation. Yours will naturally rebel against routine and there's little point trying to force him to do anything: he'll just refuse. (Ten minutes later, he'll demand exactly what you wanted, just to outwit you.) This crazy fireball will feel like a caged tiger until he can release all his frustrated energy through physical activity. That's why he will yell, rant or bang around the cot until he's literally able to get out of it.

Enjoy this little star's exuberant personality, his passion for life and his desire to get on with anything that's a challenge. Most of all, appeal to his sense of fair play.

STAR SECRETS

Why I'm adorable
- My unbounded energy keeps you on your toes
- I want to learn something new every day
- My antics are always fun to watch

Why I'm impossible
- I want it all now
- I cannot stand waiting for my next outing
- I'll scream if I don't get my way

My secret side
- I may be a fireball, but I'm also a bit of a softie
- Keep me entertained and I'll love you forever
- I'll always be there to help the underdog

I like
- Attracting your attention
- Quick nappy changes
- Being the centre of the universe
- Doing things that are forbidden

I don't like
- Being told what to do
- Playpens and prams
- Soppy grown-ups who say 'coochy-coochy-coo'
- Going to sleep

Let's sleep

The first few weeks will be difficult, simply because your new-born baby is passionate about everything in life – except going to sleep. Trying to force her into any kind of routine will be difficult, although she will eventually instigate one herself. Her restless desire for action will be obvious from the moment she comes into the world: you can almost hear her say, 'Hey, this is a great place to explore, who needs sleep?' But in the early days she'll be unable to get too far and will thrash around in your arms until she finally drops off to sleep out of boredom.

Once she is able to bop around in her baby bouncer, help her to get as much physical and mental exercise as she can through play. Let her join in with giggly bedtime stories, and don't creep around the place or she'll be sure she's missing out. Remember, your rough-and-tumble baby will always eventually drop from sheer exhaustion.

Aries babies respond well to make-believe characters. Tell yours that 'Mr Sleep' is one of her best friends – he's the one who gives her all that energy and when she wakes up she'll be refreshed and raring to go again.

Let's eat

You will always know when this little angel is hungry: he'll simply bellow for food. The one consolation is that his appetite is one of the healthiest in the zodiac. Weaning him off the breast or bottle won't be difficult, because he wants to grow up fast, but you may fight over when he eats, what he eats and how he goes about it. Your little fireball loves to chuck food around just to tease you, and the more you say no, the more he'll do it.

Survive food wars by making mealtimes fun. Remember, he adores beating you at your own game: balance his plastic spoon on your head, dip it in his puréed carrot and then eat it yourself. He'll be impressed, and will usually want to prove that he can do it better than you! As he begins to toddle he'll probably climb down from the chair to stir up trouble. Teach him about healthy competition and see who can stay longest at the table and eat all their food. The prize is his favourite ice cream. He loves to win and will adore the praise you give him every time – which means you can relax.

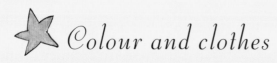 # Colour and clothes

Aries girl

The big, wide world is an exciting place, so introduce baby Aries to the bold colours that are in harmony with her own bright outlook on life. Use hot colours in the nursery – sizzling reds, tangy yellows and spicy oranges. Even if the walls are a softer tone, liven up the decoration with balloons, murals and mobiles. She will love friendly tigers and dragons, fantasy animals, wizards and heroes adorning her curtains and bedding. Play jingly music and nursery rhymes to keep this wide-awake angel amused, and once she's toddling she will adore interactive bedtime stories where she can gurgle, shout and laugh herself to sleep.

First layettes are best kept to warm yellows and citrus colours to enhance her fun-loving spirit. She will be a boisterous baby so make sure she has plenty of bib shorts and a large selection of colourful T-shirts – essential for all that playing with mud, food and running around. It won't be long before she knows which clothes are her favourites and you will find her changing two or three times a day. You will certainly never be short of washing to do.

Aries boy

The Aries boy demands lights, camera and action around
him full time. Opt for bright colours on nursery walls,
such as sunflower yellows and bold splashes of red.
A bright frieze with a parade of fiery images –
friendly dragons, smiling tigers, and sunshine places
will bring a smile to his face when he wakes early in
the morning. Variety is the key, so choose gentler
colours for beds, bedding and curtains. Try stripy
blues, or snazzy patterns, and change the theme
now and again. He'll adore revolving night-lights
and mobiles hung above his cot with dancing clowns
and circus animals – he'll dream of taming lions before long.

Keep first layettes to apricot, russet and sunny yellow to complement his
bright little personality. This is one hothead: from morning until night you
are bound to have at least two changes of clothes as he throws food around
and smears paint all over his bib shorts. He will grow out of his clothes
quicker than most, running around naked when it's warm enough, and he'll
not care what he looks like. He's all boy, so sporty T-shirts and hard-wearing
outfits suit him best.

Let's play

Your spirited baby is ready for constant stimulation. Even before she can sit up, little Aries will be kicking about, waving her arms and snatching at things. Act the clown and throw soft balls around the nursery to make her chuckle. No playpens please: this little bundle of energy hates to be confined! Huge cuddly toys, baby bouncers, walkers, activity cubes, sponge balls and building blocks are her favourite things.

Through play, this little mite will begin to understand about the healthy competition that's in her nature. Encourage building-block competitions with others and direct her energy into achieving her best. If she sees her virtuous little Virgo pal build a brick tower nearly ten blocks high, far better that she chooses to build one with twelve. Repressing that competitive spirit would result in her bashing the Virgo empire down!

This one will never be shy in company, and adores older family members spoiling her with presents, kisses and praise. She'll soon prove she's a natural leader and independent to boot. Use intelligent discipline to teach her to see the difference between bossiness and being admired as a self-starter. She'll soon realize she's not the only princess in the sandpit, but maybe, just maybe, she'll be the queen one day.

Tantrums and crocodile tears

This is one baby who will kick up a fuss about anything he doesn't want to do. New-born Aries will scream for food, a nappy change or just out of sheer frustration. Expect shrieks and tantrums when he's not getting his way and always remember that he needs huge hugs from you afterwards. With his innate sense of fairness, and your guidance, your baby will quickly learn the difference between what's acceptable and what's not. If he plays up, divert his attention with positive action. Play the clown until the rage turns to laughter then add a dash of firm but gentle discipline and tell him he's loved for being the bright star he is.

Botties, potties and bath time

The nappy is on, the nappy is off. It's on his head, it's on his toes. Your courageous little bundle is a great escape artist, and the first thing he'll discover is how to get out of the biggest restriction in his early life – the nappy. He will probably have the potty on his head too before long, and he'll be the first among his tiny pals to use it properly. Bath time is action time for this one: he'll adore splashing you, the walls, family, visitors and all.

What baby Aries wants most from you

From an early age, your little angel wants to know she's the only star in your life. If she can see that you have only eyes for her, she can begin to develop her own highly independent streak. The problem is, that she'll also be quick to discover that other family members are just as important to you as she is. That's when she'll start competing for your love and affection. Channel her competitive spirit through positive play and she'll realize you're on her side.

This one thrives in an environment where there is always something happening, or one in which she can make things happen herself. Her chuckles and screams of delight or frustration are simply her way of communicating that she wants to be boss. Teach her that self-confidence is invaluable in the world, but it's also important to be thoughtful and caring towards others.

Make every day an exciting one by introducing something 'new' into her world. She's eager to learn and you can help her to be the challenging little star that she is by exposing her to all kinds of active stimulation. Whether it's a different toy to play with or a surprise visit to the playground in the pushchair, this little hothead needs noise, fun and excitement to keep her busy mind occupied and to channel her high energy levels.

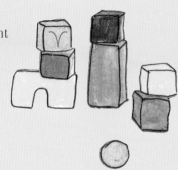

The ideal parent for Aries is adventurous, entertaining and full of confidence, someone who indulges in all kinds of action-packed games. But how do you live up to that if you happen to be a tidy Virgo who prefers peace and quiet? You can use your strengths to make the most of her courageous streak: praise her stunts, and encourage good deeds. So, for the Virgo mum who is proud of her clean kitchen but has a little Aries who throws food over the floor, remember that she adores grabbing your attention and you adore keeping order. Solution? Winner of the cleaning game gets the biggest hugs.

Baby Aries wants more than anything to be boss, and you must take care not to become a slave. If you let your baby think she can get away with anything, she soon will! Gently control her assertiveness with humour and loving discipline. She needs to be inspired and she wants to be loved for her honesty, courage and self-confidence. Teach her to turn wilfulness into willingness, and she'll be your best friend for life.

Taurus

APRIL 20 TO MAY 20

Laid-back and affectionate, I'm the most smiley baby around. I'll give you an easy life as long as you give me one too!

Look at me!

This little angel has greater determination and inner strength than appears on the surface. Placid, sleepy and responsive to simple routines, this earthy baby likes all the best home comforts. From the word go, she'll drift off in your arms and bless you with her charming gurgles and sweet smiles. So where is all that dogged persistence? Could this little bundle of joy really be as stubborn as they say? By the time she's weaned, you'll begin to realize that when she wants something badly enough she'll get it one way or another.

Patient and serene, this one needs to feel in touch with the material world. Her tactile senses are very important, and she responds to baby massage, music, warmth, beauty and nature. Little Taurus is security-conscious, and family stability really matters to her. Routines, follow-through, continuity and forward planning will help her develop into the warm, sensuous lover of beauty, people and all things natural that she's destined to be. Above all, this little mite has a heart of gold: she's loyal and loving, but remember that she needs to feel valued too. Support her choices and indulge her in the simple pleasures of life – you'll be rewarded with a strong, caring and realistic child.

STAR SECRETS

Why I'm adorable
- I just love cuddling up to you
- I care about nature and animals
- There's always a twinkle in my eye

Why I'm impossible
- I get possessive about my toys
- I'm very strong-willed
- You just can't get me out of bed

My secret side
- My greatest fear is a new situation
- I just want the simple pleasures in life
- I need a lot of sleep

I like
- Being tucked up at night
- Teddy bears
- Flopping around in big comfy sofas
- Lullabies and musical toys

I don't like
- Travelling or moving home
- Noisy crowds of people
- Changing my routine
- Sharing my sweets

Let's sleep

Early on, you might wonder why your baby sleeps so much. Is he unwell? Should you wake him? The simple answer is that the Taurus baby adores the land of nod. Although he'll want a regular sleeping routine, he's liable to doze off when you least expect it – taking catnaps in the car, power dozes in his pushchair and always looking forward to being snuggled up and sung to in the same bed every night.

Long before you believe it possible, he'll sleep right through the night, as long as he's had a good meal and plenty of hugs from you. The chances are he'll wake at the same time every morning – usually when hunger calls! And he'll be upset by a change of plan. Say you go out for 'adult time', leaving a babysitter who lets him play for an hour longer or puts him to bed earlier than usual. This is likely to make him grumpy, because routine provides him with a sense of security and he sees a break from it as a big threat.

Don't disturb him when he's asleep, provide him with the warmth and comfort of good bed covers, soothing massages and big kisses, and he'll repay you with true affection and contentment.

Let's eat

If your newborn could indulge in a gourmet meal from day one, she would. Ravenous and loving every mouthful, you won't have trouble weaning this one, and it's worth introducing her to more solid foods earlier than other babies. Taurus babies find their greatest pleasure in the basic necessities of life: solid food means a full tummy and utmost contentment.

As soon as she starts getting fretful about the bottle or breast, tempt her with healthy foods such as yogurt, honey and fruit purées. She's prone to getting very attached to her favourite foods, which usually include the things that are not good for her, and may stubbornly refuse to eat some wonderful new concoction you took all morning to prepare.

As with her sleeping pattern, routine feeding is essential to keep this one happy, so be sure to include flavours and textures she likes. The appearance of her food also matters to her, as does the look of her plastic cup, spoons, tablemat and bib. Try presenting new foods in pretty patterns on the plate to appeal to this strong aesthetic sense. Do keep an eye on her diet, though, as she is easily tempted by sweet, sticky things.

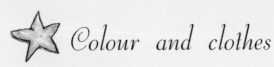 # *Colour and clothes*

Taurus boy

Earthy, sensual colours suit this little character and, above all, the nursery should reflect the comfort and luxury-loving nature of his personality. Make it look as if he's living in a palace even if your budget is tight. For walls and ceilings opt for spring greens or soft sky blues. For bed covers and cot bumpers, choose complementary colours such as lemon yellow or warm apricot. He'll adore a mural or wall frieze of farmyard scenes. He likes to move around in bed, so don't dress him in tight-fitting baby-grows or tuck him in too tight!

Keep first layettes simple in soft blues or pastel greens. Once he's up and about he likes to look good and has an eye for beauty and quality. Make sure his all-in-ones, T-shirts and dungarees are perfectly ironed, colour-coordinated and ready to be seen in all the best places. Even if he's just going to play in the sandpit or help you out in the kitchen, smart, tasteful, quality clothes make him feel good about himself. By the time he's toddling, visits to the local baby department could become a battle of wills. Be prepared to listen and adapt: he has a sense of fashion and style, and knows what suits him!

Taurus girl

Your little star is happiest surrounded by natural fabrics, pretty objects and images of nature. Even as a newborn, she'll respond to earthy colours on her nursery walls – soft blues, greens and warm spring yellows. Matching schemes for bedding, curtains or furniture will instil a sense of peace and tranquillity at bedtime. Make sure you choose skin-friendly fabrics for covers, quilts and sleeping bags, because she is very sensitive. Hang pretty fabric lanterns for soft lighting in the evening and leave a glow-light on in case she wakes up in the night. Wall friezes or stick-on borders should include flower, plant or animal themes. And she'll just love a spinning mobile of furry creatures above her cot.

First layettes should be soft pastels – lavender blue or pea green – to complement her earthy, placid nature. By the time she's pulling on her own socks, she'll like looking good in neat little pinafore dresses, snazzy tops and trendy dungarees. Baby Taurus has a shrewd sense of taste so let her make some choices of her own. If she wants to throw on that old shawl, wear her striped jumper and kick around in her wellies, let her. Her fashion sense is as determined as her common sense.

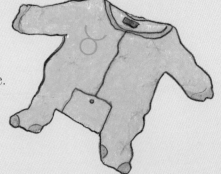

Let's play

New-born Taurus loves to touch his own ears, suck his toes and thrust his legs around during nappy changes. The physical sensation of towel, nappy and clothes is sometimes too much for his sensitive skin, so let him thrash around in his birthday suit. Once he begins to walk, he'll love to toddle around naked on warm sunny days.

He adores building bricks, creative toys, farmyard sounds and making sandcastles. He jiggles and jives around to music too, burbling and singing, dancing and clapping along with glee. He will help you stack saucepans in the kitchen, or will roll his own pastry – remember you've got a chef in the making here. Taurus is not a loner, but he does prefer small groups of little friends to noisy, rough-and-tumble play. He takes a long time to trust people and hates being poked or held by people he doesn't really know.

'That's mine' is one of the first things this little mite will want to say. Teach him through play to share his toys with his family and friends, and explain to him that his old teddy may pop off to visit other people for twenty minutes, but will always come back to the friend he loves the most.

Tantrums and crocodile tears

This little bundle has her limits and will scream if her routine is broken, although peace reigns again as soon as the pleasures of life have been restored. Temper tantrums are a rarity, but she'll rant and rave when she really feels that life isn't easy. Soothing music, a gentle massage and big cuddles will have her smiling again. Once she starts to sit up, she'll quickly learn to pout when she wants something badly enough. 'I want strawberry jelly, not new lemon!'. Banish the tears with a huge wobbly jelly she can stick her fingers in. Gradually she'll test out the new flavour herself and will probably even like it. Show her that the new is just as much fun as the tried and trusted.

Botties, potties and bath time

Nappy changing is an opportunity to let your baby do her own workout. Touching her toes and blowing raspberries will introduce her to her body and what each bit does! The potty will be welcome – your little star doesn't like being in a mess – and she'll also enjoy her bath-time routine to the full. This is one little baby who adores being wrapped up in big fluffy towels, then hugged and dried all at the same time.

What baby Taurus wants most from you

Try to keep the home environment a place of beauty, order and tranquillity. The ideal parent is a big-hearted, honest and generous person – someone who is warm, strong and consistent in his or her moods, ways and lifestyle. She loves being surrounded by the familiar, so favourite snuggle bunnies, comforters and soft-toy 'friends' will all make her feel secure when you have to leave her with a babysitter. She takes her time, and hates being hassled to learn something before it suits her. That's why she needs understanding, tolerance and, above all, patience from you.

The right kind of love is about closeness, home comforts, structured play and routine. But not all parents are made this way. If you are not a homely, routine-loving person yourself, how do you combine both your own personal wants with a baby who demands continuity and the simple pleasures of life? If you're a restless Sagittarian, for example, with a busy working life, moving house often or changing your mind at the last minute, you should be prepared for a battle of wills. Compromise is, of course, one solution. Somehow find a routine that suits you both, and always show her that you are there for her. Little Taurus needs to feel she is of value – that she's loved for her strength of character and adored for her loving, down-to-earth personality.

Nurturing this little star is actually quite easy, as long as you introduce her to the new and the different with patience and, most importantly, let her make her own choices about when she'll try them out. For example, you might be a competitive Aries who wants your baby to start toddling before any of your friends' babies. Forcing her to crawl when she'd rather be sitting around watching the world go by will only make her dig her heels in. Rather, encourage her to watch people playing. Take her to the gym with you or to the school races. If you have a pet, she'll soon catch on that it's more fun to play with the dog or cat if she can move around, instead of waiting for it to come to her. With her uncanny ability to work out how to produce the best results in the shortest possible time, she'll probably be thinking 'Hey, what's the point of crawling when I can just get up and walk?!'

Gemini

MAY 21 TO JUNE 20

There are two of me, the mischievous one and the intelligent one, but you'll never know which I'm going to be next. That's why I'm so much fun to have around.

Look at me!

This is one cheeky, mercurial little star who thrives on variety and entertainment, burbling, chatting and bouncing around the place – at times it may even seem as if you have two babies under one roof. Born under the sign of the twins, little Gemini has two sides to his nature. One is lively, dextrous and quick to learn, the other is elusive, scattered and restless. He's changeable, charming, and learns very early on how to get his way without upsetting anyone.

Even when he first opens his eyes, you'll realize this little mite is keen to find out what's going on around him. Life is an adventure for the Gemini soul, and he's also a born mimic. Bright as a button, he needs constant mental challenge and stimulus – just as you're about to give him a lovely hug he's already rolled over to play with his new soft toy. Later, once your baby is toddling, he can be a bit elusive – now you see him, now you don't. He is hard to pin down and it can be difficult to know what to expect next. The art of dealing with this little character is to expect the unexpected!

STAR SECRETS

Why I'm adorable
- I'm really quick to learn and curious about everything
- When I mimic your friends it makes you giggle
- I can do more than two things at once

Why I'm impossible
- I get bored and restless easily
- I leave all my toys lying around
- A bit of a chameleon, you just can't work me out

My secret side
- I'm fascinated by the world and want to explore it
- Talk to me like a grown-up and I'll adore you
- I'm a bit of an amateur psychologist

I like
- Chatting to myself
- Talking to everyone else
- Books, maps, words and rhymes
- Going out on visits and shopping

I don't like
- Strict mealtimes
- Slobbery kisses from adults
- Finishing things
- Having to choose what to do

Let's sleep

Falling asleep in your arms after a soothing feed isn't exactly Gemini's style. She is so curious about the world that the last thing she wants is to nod off. Your new-born star won't have a routine sleeping pattern, so be prepared for wakeful nights and catching up in the days. Help her to get to sleep by telling stories, singing lullabies and reading books together.

This is one baby who adores musical mobiles dangling above the cot and if you make bedtime a fun time, she'll look forward to the fact that come the dawn – and she will wake early – there'll be a new day full of fascinating things to do. Early on, colourful board books with plenty of big words are great for pre-bedtime winding down. When she's toddling, leave soft toys in the cot for early morning wake-ups.

Gemini responds well to simple explanation. By the time she's talking and walking, instead of just saying 'time for bed' explain why it's important to sleep. When she asks 'Why?' the next time, your answer should be: 'Because all those bubbling thoughts in your head need to have a rest too. And then they'll be even more exciting tomorrow!'

Let's eat

Don't assume that you can find an easy routine for feeding your Gemini baby. After all, he's far more interested in what's going on around him than in what happens on the inside. Make mealtimes playful occasions. While he's breast- or bottle-feeding, distract your little clown with fun wrist rattles, talk or sing to him or tell him nursery rhymes. He loves the sound of your voice and wants more than anything to communicate. Play finger games, make silly faces and, while his mind is occupied, his metabolism will do the rest.

Once he's on solids, things get easier because you can make food interesting. Hunger pangs will arrive when you're on the move and it's a good idea to be prepared with snacks like bananas, sticks of carrot and plain biscuits to encourage gum chewing and teeth nibbling. Help baby Gemini to develop a healthy eating pattern by introducing new foods as often as possible. Arrange fresh fruit and vegetables into silly faces, pretend the spoon is a train going into a tunnel (his mouth), or lay the table the wrong way round and ask him to help you get it right. He'll love proving he knows the right way to do it!

⭐ Colour and clothes

Gemini girl

Frivolous and scatty, little Gemini is more interested in what's going on in the world, than fancy wallpapers and which colour she ought to be wearing. This won't present too much of a problem, because she'll happily adapt to anything in the early days. For the nursery choose light, airy colours, such as buttercup yellows, bluebell and thistle blues, ivory and stone to enhance her light-hearted little spirit. Your mentally alert little star isn't too fond of blackout time, so make sure you use a fun revolving or musical night-light, or a mobile with wonderful dangling funny faces and animals to watch as she drifts off to sleep.

Keep first layettes to simple pastels, whites and creams, and ensure you have unfussy all-in-ones for quick changing. She gets bored with all that unfastening and fastening! As ambivalent about her clothes as she is about her nursery, she's also happy to wear unisex gear, and hates to look too girly. Once she's toddling, be prepared for frequent dressing and undressing dramas: one minute your changeable Gemini will be pointing at her hard-wearing dungarees, the next she'll want the pretty party frock she refused to wear the day before.

Gemini boy

He's as bright as a button, so maintain the
same kind of sparkling atmosphere in the
nursery. Your little ray of sunshine will thrive
on yellows and complementary denim and
cornflower blue colours on the walls. He won't
like fussy wallpapers or sweet little bunnies
everywhere. Use mix-and-match bedding, stripy
cot bumpers and an array of alphabet letters or figures on friezes and
borders. Keep curtains or blinds light and breezy, and provide fun night-
lights for after dark. Mobiles can be hung everywhere, and are great in the
early days to keep him amused as he dozes off for a daytime nap.

First layettes can be bright yellows, pastel greens or simple whites. Once
he's trundling around, he'll prefer easy, unfussy clothes that don't restrict
him. He's not particularly bothered about how he looks, but he doesn't like
to stand out from the crowd either. Khaki, stone, beige and blue are his
favourites, and he'll adore jazzy tops and the odd bright pair of socks that
reflect his mischievous streak. His fascination for all things includes the
clothes shop. He'll grab sweaters, T-shirts and funky fashionable finery, but
he'll probably never wear anything he chooses: why worry about clothes
when there's the whole wide world to explore?

Let's play

Even when tiny the adult world fascinates this curious little angel and she will spend plenty of time watching you. Sit her in the baby bouncer in front of a mirror and tell her about the little girl she can see there. From the word go you can play finger games, toe games and most of all talk, talk, talk to her. Once this lover of words and making connections starts to babble, she'll also ask 'Why?' more than most other babies. Explain why the sky is blue, the grass green and why eating is good for her quick-fire brain.

She may be fast to learn, but she's not that keen on finishing the things she starts, so be prepared for building blocks left scattered around the floor! But give her a shoebox, a wooden spoon and a cotton reel, and she'll have no trouble creating her own fun. This little character is naturally dextrous, and she'll beat the drum, read a book and pretend to phone granny all at the same time.

When it comes to making friends, this is one sociable little soul. Encourage visitors, family outings and new little friends whenever you can. She'll charm even the most staid adults, bringing joy to everyone around.

Tantrums and crocodile tears

Like any new-born baby, this one will cry if he's hungry or needs a nappy change. Your restless little bundle will also chortle, babble to himself, even whimper now and again but, luckily, if you can keep the communication channels open, you'll be blessed with sweet gurgles rather than blood-curdling screams. Temper tantrums are only likely if he's bored or left alone in a playpen, where he'll feel like a caged bird. Divert his attention and take him out into the garden, blow bubbles into the sky and he'll clap with delight.

Botties, potties and bath time

Nappy changing routines won't be welcome unless you can keep your little star amused. Hang brightly coloured mobiles over the changing area, or play 'this little piggy' and continue the rhyme to include how 'this little piggy' also had to have his nappy changed. Toilet training will be challenging. He's far more interested in who's just come through the front door than responding to nature's call. Encourage him to treat the potty like one of his friends and make it a playful occasion rather than an order. Bath time is fun time. He's not a great splasher, but he will happily chat to a plastic duck for hours.

What baby Gemini wants most from you

The perfect loving parent for this little mite is one who is logical, listens, talks, encourages him to be curious about the world and is as playful in spirit as he is. Words, books, funny games and social interaction will make him feel the world is his oyster and will help develop his unique potential as a socially adept and fun-loving child. But not all parents are made this way. If you're a complex Scorpio or a kitchen-efficient Cancer you might find his constant questioning, superficial babble and cheeky playfulness all very exhausting. Let him play with magnetic alphabet letters on the fridge door while you're preparing the meals; encourage him to learn to read; make time to pop down to the local shops. He adores sitting in the shopping trolley and seeing the world in action, and this diverse and sometimes hard-to-understand little soul, will reward you with the easy-going love and affection he seeks for himself.

Big hugs may not be his style, but effective communication is. The right kind of love for this little star is providing a varied environment in which people talk, listen and learn. The only problem is that baby Gemini likes to steal the show and never stops talking. Suggest that if he listens to what others say too, he'll discover even more exciting things in life to babble about to his friends and family.

Once walking, this one needs plenty of activity to release that pent-up mental energy. Give him opportunities to perform a number of activities all at once. Channel his restlessness with regular social interaction. Even if you're a solitary type, this is one little creature who needs to flit from friends to family and from one place to another – whether in the buggy, a baby walker or on his favourite toy car.

Encourage his agile, dextrous talents and if he's left-handed or ambidextrous – as many Geminis are – help him to develop this innate skill. Never try to pigeonhole him: he's far shrewder than you think. The Gemini personality is multifaceted and, like any diamond, it takes time to know all the different faces of your twin-souled treasure. He may have a restless, dual personality, but he's also got the wings of a free bird. Treasure them.

Cancer

JUNE 21 TO JULY 22

I'm a bit of a dreamer but I love everyone who is part of the family. I have an amazing memory, and my imagination knows no bounds.

Look at me!

Baby Cancer needs to feel at home in your house. Acutely sensitive to the myriad energies around her, this little creature knows that there are very beautiful things to experience and discover in life, but she finds the world a threatening place. She thrives on routine, hearing your voice and being as close to you as possible. Little Cancer needs more than anything to feel secure and to develop a sense of belonging. She almost comes into the world with a frown on her face. What is this place? Could it be as blissful as it was in your womb? How will she deal with it?

Initially she'll be shy and clingy, but give her time to get to know your family and friends and she'll blossom into the compassionate person she's destined to be. Her moods will swing from incredible laughter at her big brother's antics to tears and sadness when she sees a lost dog. There will certainly be times when she hides under the bedclothes or tucks herself behind your legs. But she'll also enjoy the company of her family and, once toddling, will be the most considerate of souls. Her imagination knows no bounds so let her babble away at the man in the moon.

STAR SECRETS

Why I'm adorable
- I'm intuitive, sensitive and kind
- I care about animals and people
- Once I can toddle, I love helping in the kitchen

Why I'm impossible
- I go all moody for no apparent reason
- I don't like it when you leave me alone
- You won't get me out of the bath in a hurry

My secret side
- Don't rush me, I take one day as it comes
- I'm quite a tough cookie when I want to be
- I need a secret place for all my toys

I like
- Being held and snuggling up to you
- Collecting soft toys
- Fairy tales and my imagination
- Being told secrets

I don't like
- Noisy parties and boisterous friends
- Going away from home and travelling
- Getting up in the morning
- Being held by strangers

Let's sleep

Whether snuggling up close or dropping off in your arms after a feed, new-born Cancer is one of the easiest babies to get to sleep, as long as he knows you're close by. Your little bundle still carries a strong resonance of the time in your womb where he was safe from the outside world and comforted by being close to you. He has a hard time separating from you, so let him fall asleep beside you early on, or rock him gently in his cot and play soft music. Give him warmth, comfort and a cot that feels as safe and secure to him as you do.

As he gets older and more alert to the world, this one will enjoy lullabies, a bath before bedtime and a kiss from all the family. He'll quickly establish a sleep pattern that includes a good nap during the day. Once he's toddling, he'll love getting ready for bed, then spending a little time in your arms while you tell him his favourite fairy tale. Waking him up could prove difficult: he loves sleep so much that, if you're an early riser, or ready to dash off about town, you need to give him time to shake off his doziness!

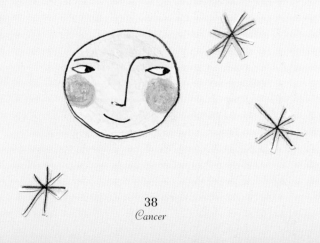

Let's eat

This little character won't be in much of a hurry to give up the breast or bottle. Being close to you gives her a great sense of security, and there's no point forcing her into highchairs, eating solids or wholesome cooking until she's ready for it. She may also be very unpredictable about her feeding patterns. She's hungry one day, but whimpering and refusing to eat the next. She's ruled by the moon, so changes like the tide.

Make sure eating time is a quiet time. A noisy environment will only put her off. Her sensitive nature is in tune with what's going on around her. If other children are crashing around the place, she'll make a noise too. Encourage her to try new foods when she's in one of her hungry moods. Small portions or snack foods suit her metabolism and include fresh soft fruits, the odd biscuit or toast and jam. By the time she's toddling, don't abandon her to a highchair. This is one little star who adores sitting at the table as part of the family. Survive her faddy tastes and unpredictable eating habits by encouraging her to help you in the kitchen. She'll love stirring up your sponge-cake mix and then licking the bowl!

⭐ *Colour and clothes*

Cancer boy

This character feels most at home in warm, simple, unchanging surroundings, so resist the temptation to redecorate the nursery in the first few years of his life. Tranquil pastels on the walls – lavender, peach or softest violet – complemented with richer tones of blue and green in accessories or bedding, will give him the watery sense of security he needs around him. Choose natural or skin-safe fabrics for sheets, quilts and mattresses. He is a sensitive little soul and needs the utmost comfort. Around the room, have a place for his rows of soft toys, and borders of dolphins, funny fish and whales.

Stick to softest blues and greens for first layettes. Once he's more outgoing and secure in the big wide world, he'll prefer action clothes in the morning, and looking good when on visits. This little creature wants the best in life, so always opt for quality over quantity. Choose coastal colours ranging from the muted green and greys of gentle waves on the beach, to the deepest blues of the ocean. He's a water babe, don't forget, and needs to feel safe hiding behind his protective outer shell.

Cancer girl

Your sensitive little girl needs to be cuddled and cosseted, so ensure that her bedding and nightwear remind her of the warmth and closeness she had in the womb. Use soft, sensitive fabrics and soothing wall colours – soft lilac, lavender, warm rose or gentle dove grey. This sleepy, but restless, little star will thrive surrounded by images of the sea, but will also like fairy tale characters and pretty friezes of animals or a string of teddy bears dangling above her cot. Hang a rose quartz crystal in the window to energize the quality of closeness and attract 'love' energy into the nursery.

Keep first layettes to soft pinks or pastel blues. She's a real little girl, so include a range of hats or bonnets in her toddler wardrobe and a kaleidoscope of colourful sweaters, T-shirts and pinafore dresses. She has an eclectic taste for clothes and, whether a bib suit or a skirt, she adores every piece of clothing as if it were her favourite snuggle bunny. She'll cling to the all-in-one she wore when she was four months old so invest in several pairs of pretty pyjamas or a smart dressing gown to snuggle up in – one, two, or even three sizes larger.

Let's play

Security-conscious Cancer enjoys soft fist rattles, cuddly companions and a baby bouncer with a view of you in the kitchen. Introduce him to the home so that he really gets to know and trust it: carry him in a sling and show him paintings, pets, flowers and images that gradually show him it is safe to play away from your lap. All babies have a horror of being separated from their parents and this is most apparent in little Cancer's interaction, or lack of it, with others. He's not a social creature and takes time to trust even his granny, let alone strangers. Don't force him to play with little Thomas next door because it will 'do him good': it is more likely to end in tears.

His toys are possessions that he cares, and sometimes worries, about. Although it's important to teach him about sharing, suggest that his 'special' teddies, bunnies or collection of soft toys are kept in a place only he knows about. The toys that are on display downstairs are the ones he can teach other people to look after. Eventually he'll realize that when his train disappears into the kitchen with his older brother it won't have gone forever.

Tantrums and crocodile tears

Naturally sensitive, little Cancer will cry if she's restless and crotchety. By the time she's toddling her anger will arise mostly from a fear of being separated from her favourite things (which includes you). Whether she sucks her thumb or fiddles with the battered label of a soft toy, indulge in her need and you'll avoid the tears. She'll turn to manipulative tears the moment she feels vulnerable. Create a diversion: say something like 'Where's Barney the dog/cat/cuddly toy? Let's go and find him.' The fact that something is separated from you both will give her the motivation to go find it and make sure it's as safe as she is.

Botties, potties and bath time

Your water baby loves a soothing, calm bath time. Play trickling water games and gently splash her toes. Take care washing her hair: she hates getting water in her eyes. Nappies will irritate her, because she has sensitive skin, but don't push her into toilet training. She'll take her time to trust that potty, which seems to have a magical ability to follow her around the house. Tell her the fairies at the bottom of the garden left it for her – she might just believe you. If they use a potty, then why shouldn't she?

What baby Cancer wants most from you

Like any baby, little Cancer needs physical love, warmth, comfort and a home in which he feels safe and secure. But he thrives on emotional nurturing too. He has to feel that you are there for him and understand his moods, intuitive world, nostalgic memories and his attachment to possessions. Give him all the support and assurance you can, and remember he does have a tendency to take everything very personally. If you are a dynamic Sagittarian or rational Aquarian you might find his clinginess a little overwhelming. Take care: he fears rejection most of all. As he begins to toddle, provide him with a tent or a Wendy house so that he can make his own home. Understand he loves collecting things, is in touch with the magical world of nature and responds to gentle guidance rather than negative discipline.

He's a born 'carer' himself, so encourage him to look after his favourite toy, protect his teddy bear and help you in the kitchen. Make sure your home is a calm, peaceful place. He'll be very attached to you, which means he's also very reliant on you. If you do have to leave him with someone else, make sure you also leave a bit of yourself so that he knows you're coming back. Give him a scarf that has a hint of your perfume dabbed on or a book you always read together at bedtime. Slowly introduce him to doing things like drying himself at bath time and develop his sense of independence so that he can grow into the strong, caring, emotionally self-sufficient child that he is destined to be.

Most of all, this one needs to know that he won't be rejected for his failures. If he does take time to ask for what he wants, or goes about doing something in a very roundabout way, give him confidence in himself by letting him know that he's making good progress too. Whatever he produces in play – a piece of paper ripped up or an imaginative story about his snuggle bunny – listen, learn and praise him. This is one child whose intuition and sensitive nature can be channelled into all kinds of creative fields. Teach him to express his sensitivity instead of feeling engulfed by it.

Leo

JULY 23 TO AUG 22

Extrovert and spirited, I want to be the star of the show.
I'm also generous and loyal, and give the biggest kisses around.

Look at me!

There's something about this newborn that is incredible, but true: he actually seems to be smiling from the moment he's born. This fun-loving little rogue simply wants to get on in life right from the word go. With enthusiasm for everything and everyone, people warm quickly to his exuberant personality. By the time little Leo is out and about in his pushchair, strangers will gather round to admire his big smile and his centre-stage presence. This is the kind of showman who will toss his rattle to the floor for attention or knock over tins in the supermarket to create some drama in a dull world.

All he wants is to be the star of the show, to be the most special little person in your life and to dazzle others with his madcap antics. This is one baby who really will shout 'look at me' once he can talk. The only problem is that you're likely to hear it a million times a day, so be prepared for mischief from morning until bedtime! Encourage Leo's generosity among friends and help him develop his gregarious side. He's destined to be the shiniest star around, so guide him to share the greatest gift he has to offer to the world: love.

STAR SECRETS

Why I'm adorable
- I may be a little lion, but I'm also a pussycat
- I love meeting new people
- My smile lights up your life

Why I'm impossible
- I'm the one on the throne, and that's that
- What a show-off I am!
- I love making a mess of mealtimes

My secret side
- I boast and brag but I'm actually very insecure
- I want you to tell me you love me every day
- When I grow up I want to be a celebrity

I like
- Looking glamorous
- Dragons, adventure, magicians and heroes
- People who smile
- Being praised

I don't like
- Not being noticed
- Having to sit still for too long
- Grumpy grown-ups who don't laugh
- Waiting for dinner

Let's sleep

Make Leo feel that going to sleep is something she
does better than anyone else. Early on she may
not settle easily, nights may be chaotic and she
won't like being left on her own. Lullabies,
soothing massages or simply holding her close to
you until she drops off are techniques you'll have
to employ. Once baby Leo is toddling, she'll begin to
find her own sleeping pattern – which, of course, may be contrary to
the one you would like her to have! This little bundle of energy has
so much vitality that she simply crashes out, whether in the middle
of her playmates, or on your friend's carpet.

She won't enjoy bedtime if she's being left out of the family fun downstairs,
and you'll find yourself facing the tactical 'I want more milk, I want my other
teddy, I want...' game. Make her believe that she's the star of a nightly 'sleep
show': her room is her palace, her toys are her entourage, the bed is her
own magic stage from which she can rule her kingdom. Massive hugs and
kisses from you and all the family will give her that sense of being the
starlet by day, but also the queen of the show come night-time.

Let's eat

Make eating every mouthful a grand comedy, with little Leo centre stage, and you'll both enjoy hours of fun. He wants to know that everyone is watching him perform so give him well-earned praise when he starts to use his plastic spoon, even if it's on his head and not in his mouth. Bright, colourful food and utensils will appeal to his flamboyant streak. He'll love anything from mashed bananas to mangoes, and is always happy to try out new foods and flavours.

Once he can talk, 'I'm hungry' is one of the phrases he'll use most. In fact, if the food looks jolly and playful he'll eat it up in no time. Once he's toddling he'll adore showing how he can get his juice or beaker from the fridge, and he'll proudly nibble on a carrot, gingerbread man or plain rusk as you whizz him around in the supermarket trolley. Praise him for all mealtime efforts, and if the kitchen is a total mess afterwards, encourage him to help you clear up. Remember he responds to being treated like royalty but, like any king of the castle, he'll also want the kitchen to be showcase material.

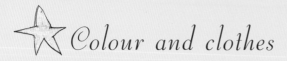

Colour and clothes

Leo girl

This fiery little angel adores the fantastic, the extravagant and the brash. Little Leo thrives in a light, bright, jolly environment so opt for saffron, wheat or golden yellows on the walls. Complement with cornflower blue, splashes of poppy red or other bold primary colours in friezes and toy displays. Have cats roaming her borders and hang fantastic paper-tiger mobiles above her cot. Add some sparkle with a true princess-style light – all glitzy and glamorous.

The first layettes should be in strong bold colours like strawberry or raspberry, sunflower yellow and warm sunset orange. Your little star is proud of her appearance. Once she's charging around the home, she'll try on your lipstick and your latest party shoes – all much more showy than baby wear. Opt for the most fashionable wardrobe, as well as the loudest and brightest. Snazzy tops, shimmery pyjamas, the odd tutu and, of course, the usual mix of bib suits and pinafore dresses in easy-care, durable fabrics for the countless paint or food spillages. Keep the ultimate 'princess' dress for special occasions. Whatever she wears, this one simply wants to shine brighter and look more beautiful than everyone else.

Leo boy

Proud and a bit of a show-off, your little Leo
will thrive in a room that is his own palace
of delights and a den for future playmates.
His surroundings must be bold, bright and
exuberant, so decorate the nursery in rich,
vibrant colours – sunshine yellow or warm
apricot. Stick stars on the ceiling, add an activity
night-light and choose circus themes for friezes and
borders. Castles, kings, crowns and treasure-island posters or
mobiles will appeal to his fantasy world. Complement all with simple
creams, whites and neutral colours for bedding, as this could be too
much for visiting grans!

For first layettes opt for yellows and soft orange. This is one rough-and-
tumble boy, so dress him in clothes that won't wear out. By the time he's
the king of the sandpit, he'll also want to show off his new outfit and maybe
even insist on choosing his own clothes. Whether in T-shirt and jeans or
smart little dungarees, he has an eye for colour coordination. It may be a
little excessive, but his creative talents could put a top fashion guru to
shame. He'll love designer labels (if you can't afford the real thing, any
label will do) because he thinks he's one of the crème de la crème.

Let's play

Little Leo is the ultimate party animal. She adores the limelight and will demand attention – basking in the glory of admiring strangers and loving family members. People are her toys. Bring in big brother or sister, uncle or aunt, granny or friendly toddler. Make faces, stick out tongues, blow raspberries, tickle and giggle together. Play peek-a-boo or simply tell her funny stories and sing nursery songs. Once she's on her feet, she'll be following you around, gurgling, chatting and demanding your attention round the clock. Make your home a magical place, so that she can imagine her nursery is the queen's chamber, the playpen full of teddies and soft toys, her loyal subjects. This little one adores admiring herself in the mirror and she'll need her own 'dressing-up' box. She wants to be a star and adores pretending that she's one of her favourite fairy tale princesses in front of an audience. Socially adept, she should be encouraged to play with toddler friends and be the generous little soul she is. Exhausting and fun to have around she thrives on adventure, action and the great outdoors. Once she's running – probably before she walks – slides, swings and climbing frames are all great activities for the star of the playground.

Tantrums and crocodile tears

If he's not centre stage he'll soon let you know about it. This is one character who has to be noticed and wants to be the boss. Early on he'll scream, sob and rant if he's hungry, bored or uncomfortable, but he'll quickly stop once he gets what he wants. His big theatrical scenes about nothing are down to the sheer frustration of not being able to communicate in grown-up vocabulary. If he does start to put on the tears, or screams in the supermarket for your undivided attention, give it to him, but help him to be thoughtful towards others too. Diversion tactics when he reaches the terrible twos are invaluable. But tantrums never last long, and if you show him you still love him for all his amateur dramatics, he'll give you a great big hug.

Botties, potties and bath time

Make nappy changes fun, giving little Leo plenty of time to kick and thrash around naked in a warm environment. He'll love showing you how he can wriggle, squirm and play with his toes. This is one hilarious character at bath time. Expect pools of water and toys all over the floor. Your baby will adore having his hair washed and splashing you in the face.

What baby Leo wants most from you

The ideal parent for this little star is bold, funny, extrovert and, at times, larger than life. You also have to prove that you love him more than anyone else in the world. A tall order if he's got other siblings and you a host of close friends. Little Leo isn't the clingy type, but he does want to be in control of his clan. His world is literally that, and he will rule both you and the household if you don't make it clear early on that, although he is a very special person, other people matter too.

Not all parents are dramatists or clowns, however. What if you're a serious Capricorn or a sensitive Cancer? This little mite prefers action, so if you're happier spending hours slaving over a hot stove or gazing into space dreaming of the perfect holiday home, be wise enough to put time aside for entertaining your baby too. Once he's sitting or rushing around in his baby walker, encourage him to bang wooden spoons on your pots and pans while you're baking bread. Or show him how to get all messed up with toddler face paints while you're studying the property magazines. When he gurgles, burbles or says 'Look at me!' do exactly that, and show him that you think he's the cleverest, most splendid or greatest performer there is with your biggest smiles and hugs.

A word of caution: avoid the temptation to treat him so much like royalty that he doesn't learn to develop his benevolent, social virtues or you'll have a bossy, controlling little star on your hands. Give him an adoring audience and soft toys to care for, and let him know every day that you love him by saying it out loud.

Little Leo is actually very insecure, which is why he strives to be the best at everything he does to ensure that others will love him. This is one special child and he knows it from the day he is born, but he needs assurances from you that it's OK to be celebrity material. Make life rich, colourful and exciting: he's destined to be a star of a very big show but, like all professionals, he must learn to respect the other stars on the stage too.

Virgo

AUGUST 23 TO SEPTEMBER 22

I have a heart of gold and always want to please you. Even if I seem rather shy, I'm brilliant with words and want to be knowledgeable about everything.

Look at me!

From the moment she's born, this little star is acutely sensitive to her physical environment. She needs a quiet, calm and orderly family life with well-planned routines. This is one little baby who is as discriminating in her choice of food, toys and surroundings as she is in people. Baby Virgo finds the big wide world a very scary place and she needs tremendous love and positive encouragement to make her feel secure. From the cot to the pushchair, she will take time evaluating every aspect of a situation. She'll scrutinize the behaviour of friends and passers-by in order to work out what they're about. This is one bright little button and once she is capable of play she will adore being surrounded by her books, crayons, bits of paper, puzzles and, of course, her organized chaos.

Help your baby to develop her verbal, creative and intellectual skills, and praise her for even the smallest achievement. She may not be an extrovert go-getter, but she does adore words and is an intellectual star in the making. She also has a wry sense of humour. Blessed with the healing touch, she will soothe your brow after a tiring day and is the kindest, most helpful child of the zodiac.

STAR SECRETS

Why I'm adorable
- I like to look cute and stay clean all the time
- I'm helpful, kind and care about animals
- Once I can talk, I say fascinating and funny things

Why I'm impossible
- I'm a very fussy eater
- My organized chaos drives you mad
- I'm very sensitive to noise, pollution and smells

My secret side
- I'm very smart and quick to psych you out
- Give me a routine and I'll thrive
- I prefer the company of grown-ups

I like
- Brand new sheets and clothes
- Looking after my imaginary friends
- Learning something new every day
- Keeping my books in order

I don't like
- Noisy people
- Changes in routine
- Dirty fingernails
- People staring at me

Let's sleep

He nods off and you tiptoe out of his nursery like a mouse. Then the door squeaks and he's awake in a flash and wailing again. This little creature is so attuned to noises, smells and things that go bump in the night that, unless you live in the middle of nowhere, it's going to be hard getting him to sleep easily right through.

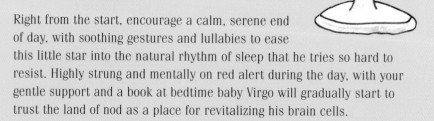

Right from the start, encourage a calm, serene end of day, with soothing gestures and lullabies to ease this little star into the natural rhythm of sleep that he tries so hard to resist. Highly strung and mentally on red alert during the day, with your gentle support and a book at bedtime baby Virgo will gradually start to trust the land of nod as a place for revitalizing his brain cells.

A strange bed, or a change in procedure, and you'll have a fretful baby on your hands. Always explain what is happening before you change a routine. This is a baby who performs best when able to make sense of whatever it is you do. By the time he's toddling and beyond, this little character will have some fascinating things to recount to you in the moments before dropping off to sleep.

Let's eat

Pernickety and cautious, your new-born Virgo might take a while to adjust to a feeding routine. Her digestive system is quite delicate, but once a routine is established she'll quickly make up for having been sensitive early on. Weaning her from the breast or bottle may need extra patience and understanding, because she's disturbed by change. Introduce solids gradually, be patient with new tastes, and offer very simple, natural or organic foods, which she'll find easier to digest and which will suit her health-conscious temperament.

Virgos prefer eating little and often to sitting down to a Sunday roast with a hoard of gobbling adults. Munching on healthy snacks – fresh carrot and celery sticks – and mealtimes in a quiet, noise-free environment will help her to enjoy the pleasures of eating. Don't get frustrated if she turns her head away or hasn't eaten exactly the right amount: she's smart enough to know when she's hungry and when she's not. And if a family member keeps offering her something she doesn't want to try, explain that she'll do so in her own time. Teach her to help lay the table to give her a sense of practical achievement.

Colour and clothes

Virgo boy

Acutely sensitive to rough, itchy materials, baby Virgo needs skin-friendly sheets, pillows and quilts or duvets. Remember to wash them in the most sensitive washing products as well. Your cool little star likes a simple, muted, almost minimalist décor. No grand colour schemes or fussy patterns, please! This one has a need for an orderly and efficient nursery – everything in its place to begin with – although he may prefer his own organized chaos later on. Choose neutral beiges, stone or cream shades for the walls, adding the odd splash of lavender, crisp green or sharp pink when it comes to the bookshelves (of which there should be many) and toy boxes.

Self-conscious from day one, little Virgo loves to be dressed in neat, unfussy clothes. Simple chic is what he needs to complement his modest but shrewd outlook on life. Opt for russets, muted stone and khaki colours, easy-to-wear bib suits and dungarees, and he'll easily blend with many a surrounding. He'll be obsessive about wearing spotless clothes, so keep a neat pile of favourite T-shirts in good supply and fill his sock drawer with immaculate matching pairs.

Virgo girl

Clean nappies, spotless all-in-ones, knickers or socks – they all have their place in baby Virgo's nursery. Her toys and colour schemes have to be ordered as well. Simple shades of pink, cream or off-white on the walls enhance the  cool, gentle environment she needs in order to feel safe and secure. Add the odd crazy giraffe or night-light and your little star will be content. Too much is too much for this little one so no flashing lights, snazzy wallpapers or clashing colours. If you want to brighten things up, include a stack of pretty picture books, an alphabet mobile or keep favourite knick-knacks (all carefully dusted) on the shelves.

Her first layettes can be as white as snow and her sheets, duvets or quilts soft, smooth and skin friendly. Toddling Virgos adore wearing clothes that have been hung outside to dry. Include smart pinafore dresses, leggings or tights if the weather is cold and have a plentiful supply of girly outfits in soft pinks, dove greys and sorbet yellows. Add little extras once she begins to have more interest in her finery – mittens, hats, party shoes, petticoats and shawls – she'll adore them and will take great pleasure from fiddling with buttons, bows and shoelaces to keep herself amused.

Let's play

Bath books, soft books, board books – they all provide baby Virgo with hours of fun. He adores being wheeled around a bookshop or having you write imaginary words on his knee when he's being changed. He may consume knowledge at the expense of his food, but that's what gives him a sense of security.

Notice the aptitude your little star has for finishing something to perfection! Make a game of tidying the kitchen or arranging his soft toys in rows of different sizes so that he can begin to put names to ideas and concepts. He'll relish scribbling with crayons, pencils and pens and will fold bits of paper into imaginary animals. Virgo babies want to be 'very good' at something, so encourage him to learn, read and use his hands. Above all, praise him for the tiniest thing: detail is all-important to this little mite.

When it comes to making friends, this one is slow to interact socially and will be very wary of strangers. He's more likely to be scrutinizing the colour of your best friend's lipstick than gurgling as she coochy-coos him in his pram! He prefers the company of just one or two equally serious-minded pals to a gaggle of fiery little souls.

Tantrums and crocodile tears

Things that distress your little angel are noise, disorder and a change in routine. Early on she'll probably cry out of tiredness because she has not slept soundly, but once good patterns have been established she'll be the sweetest and least demanding baby around. Her tantrums, albeit rare, are usually brought on by frustration and an irritation that things are not perfect: her clothes not fitting properly; an itch on her foot; a taste she doesn't like; a toy that she can't work out; and being treated like a baby! Have some respect and your little bundle will give you all the love in the world.

Botties, potties and bath time

The last thing little Virgo wants is a soiled nappy and the first thing she learns is to let you know about it. Potties will be welcome, but in her own time, so don't force her to use them just because her brother potty-trained himself at the age of 18 months! She'll adore bath time, but will hate getting water on her face or any splashing around. This is one spick-and-span little baby who loves to be washed gently, and once she can speak will probably be reminding you that it is time the bath had a clean too!

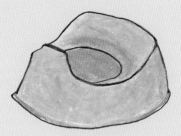

What baby Virgo wants most from you

Ritual and routine are the greatest gifts you can
give this little mite as he starts out in life. The ideal
parent is one who is observant, intellectually
fascinating, down-to-earth, quiet, unfussy and willing to let baby help
around the house. Your observations will help him to develop his own talent
for discrimination. Your amazing thoughts and ideas, your bookshelves and
your interest in everything under the sun will encourage him to learn and
to increase his ever-expanding knowledge. But are you that kind of parent?
Perhaps you're an Aries, who thrives on a busy social life, erratic mealtimes
and playing squash rather than studying the number of petals on a daisy.
In which case, you are going to need to compromise.

The right kind of home for this one is above all a quiet, organized, neat and
tidy one. A place in which people can be categorized easily by the way they
behave – big brother always goes to school at the same time, Auntie Jane
usually comes to supper on Saturdays. There is a designated time for
everything: when the clock says it's teatime,
it's teatime. Your little star's a stickler for
routine and demands equal self-discipline
in his teacher – and that's you.

The right kind of love for nurturing
your baby's own unique personality,
should revolve around encouragement:
give him plenty of praise for everything he does, set him tasks and always
bring a reward into the equation because he loves earning something for his
deeds. He will flourish in the great outdoors and loves nothing more (except
his bookshelves) than being surrounded by nature and fresh air.

Baby Virgo has little time for errors, and is always trying to correct them in
himself or finding fault with others. Teach him that the world isn't a perfect
place and that the flaws in nature are what make it very beautiful and
interesting. Always be honest and truthful – there is no duping this very
astute creature. He is giving, clever, intellectually wise and has a healer's
magical touch, but he does need to learn that love is not just black and
white – there is a little bit of mystery too.

Libra

SEPTEMBER 23 TO OCTOBER 22

Peace-loving and sweet-as-pie, I always want to please you. My cute smile lights up your life, and you can't find fault with me.

Look at me!

There he is – gurgling, smiling, almost chuckling at the world from the first moment. Being blessed with laid-back Libra is a marvellous opportunity to develop the diplomacy, charm and innate love of people that he brings to the world. How can you not be spellbound by his gaze, his sweet gentle manner? Don't be fooled! This little star knows a trick or two. Unlike the upfront 'I want' behaviour of the fiery signs, sociable Libra is well versed in the art of manipulation. He knows that compromise, charm and soft-sell tactics are the techniques that work. In fact, he usually gets what he wants in the nicest possible way.

Most of all, the charmer of the zodiac seeks approval. He knows that, if he plays the role of the perfect baby, he'll be sure to win you over, revel in your smiles and attention and still get the chocolate pudding when you'd rather give him apple purée. Difficulties arise when the time comes for him to make his mind up. Why play with building blocks when paint pots look just as interesting? Encourage him to make decisions by telling him that he can always do the other thing another day.

STAR SECRETS

Why I'm adorable
- I can charm monkeys out of trees
- I'll gurgle away to myself and won't make a fuss
- I want everyone to be as happy as I am

Why I'm impossible
- I often say yes, when I really mean no
- I take ages to decide what I want for pudding
- You have to keep my room spotless

My secret side
- I'm far more sensitive than you think
- Diplomacy is how I get my way
- I'm happiest surrounded by beautiful things and people

I like
- Looking at myself in the mirror
- Being part of a crowd
- Party clothes, art and music
- Chatting all day long

I don't like
- Being left alone
- Arguments and people who aren't fair
- Having to make a decision
- Messy people

Let's sleep

In the early days she coos and suckles, twinkles her eyes at you and seems very happy to drift off to sleep in your arms. That's because she's a people person and thrives in close contact with you. Rock her gently, smooth her back or forehead and sing her lullabies. Give her your undivided attention as she drifts off, and she's likely to sleep peacefully on her own. Otherwise you could find her in your bed every night for the next ten years! The only problem you might encounter is her waking up in the morning to find herself all alone. As she develops her social skills beyond you, favourite teddies, cuddly toys and friendly faces dangling from a mobile will all give her someone to talk to on these mornings.

By the time she's toddling, she's so keen to please you that she'll be happy to go to bed, unless of course there are family or friends socializing downstairs. Then she'll want to join in the party. Negotiate, rather than discipline. Say, 'You can stay down for an extra ten minutes, and then I'll read to you, OK?' Compromise works both ways and can be in your favour too.

Let's eat

This little mite hasn't a huge appetite, but he does adore the good things in life. He is civilized and demands clean bottles, beakers, bibs and tableware. You may have trouble getting him to feed himself, simply because it's so much easier if someone else is willing to do it. Negotiate, even if you have to resign yourself to offering a reward of ice cream if he eats up the rather dull (to him), but healthy (to you) puréed carrots. He'll be happy to please you and will realize that he can get what he wants too. Make meals sociable, harmonious occasions with no arguments. Once he's toddling show him how pleasurable eating can be by having exactly what he has. Never show distaste for, or criticize, what goes into your mouth: he'll simply copy you.

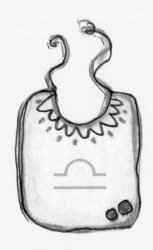

Avoid questions like, 'Would you rather have fish or chicken tonight?'. He'll take a very long time to decide, and won't like committing himself. Rather than force him to choose, gently encourage him to weigh up the possibilities with you. 'Well, I think fish would be nice because we haven't had it for a while'. Probably next time you ask him, he'll repeat the phrase verbatim, just to please you!

Colour and clothes

Libra girl

Baby Libra simply loves having the
most pretty, exquisitely tasteful things
around her. A born fashion guru, she
knows what should go where in her nursery
and how to show off and look her best. She's also a bit of a
perfectionist, so make the nursery a cosy but well-balanced blend of
colours, fabrics and toys. If one half of the room is filled with toys and
the other half empty, she'll soon feel off balance herself! For decoration,
choose light, airy colours – a palette of pastels in pink or soft yellows and
pea greens. Bring as much natural light into the nursery as you can and
add shiny mobiles or hang white crystals in the window to enhance the
fresh, breezy nature of this little creature. All these neutral tones can be
complemented with bedding and accessories of bright fuchsia, sunflower
yellow or deeper turquoise.

The first layettes should reflect her harmonious nature in gentle oyster,
stone or off-white shades. Later on, she'll laugh and make faces in

pretty hats, frivolous little dresses and the latest trends. She's
the ultimate party girl so don't stop her putting on your old
petticoat and starting a fashion all of her own.

Libra boy

Your laid-back Libra thrives in a calm, harmonious household, so make sure the nursery reflects this too. Gentle, cool, summer colour schemes suit his perfectionist, but light-hearted nature. If you have a head for heights, paint clouds on the ceiling and a sunrise with a smiley face. He'll adore funny cartoon characters on friezes, blown-up photos of family faces and posters of make-believe characters. Remember to maintain a balance, though: too much of one thing and he'll feel uncomfortable.

First layettes should be simple – white or soft pastel blues to reflect his airy personality. He's a social animal, and one who wants approval wherever he goes. Make sure you dress him in the latest style so that family members and friends comment on his trendy new sleepsuit or sporty shorts. He'll adore checking himself out in the mirror and fiddling with his hair, his wonky sleeves and buttons – 'immaculate' is his middle name. He's not a great one for real rough and tumble but, because he's usually happiest in a social whirl, choose light-fitting, casual clothes with flair. His passion for style means he'll also want to be one of the best-dressed little boys around.

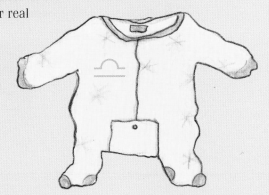

Let's play

This little socialite thrives on interactive play with others, which means you'll be in constant demand as well. Little Libra doesn't enjoy being left on her own. Encourage her to develop an imaginary 'social circle' among her soft toys, or give her a safe baby mirror and she'll chatter away to herself, making friends with the happy smiley face in the reflection. Play peek-a-boo around the kitchen table while you're preparing supper for friends, and she'll gurgle in her baby bouncer instead of whining for attention. Talk to her, show her things, point to pictures, take her in the garden and let her smell the flowers. Tickle her nose with grass, and indulge her in the world of nature, music and art.

Arrange a busy social life with family, grannies, aunts and little friends, and she'll be the perfect little hostess, keeping everyone else happy which means she'll be happy too. Encourage her make-believe world, and if she asks you about the fairies at bottom of the garden, say 'why not invite them to tea one day?' Your little star seeks the fair, the good and the beautiful and, most of all, she can find it through her imagination. So believe in it too.

Tantrums and crocodile tears

Peace-loving as baby Libra is, there are going to be times when he'll cry if things don't seem balanced or harmonious. 'It's not fair!' he'll shriek when a puzzle is too complicated. As he approaches the terrible twos, frustration at his own lack of decision-making could bring tears to his eyes. Crocodile tears are more common than tantrums, because he soon learns that a sad face can often be a very useful means of getting his way. He might be all sweetness and light, but this little diplomat wants everything to be fair in the world – he's likely to get upset if the cat can't get through the locked cat flap or if someone in the family is arguing.

Botties, potties and bath time

Splashing around in the bath is appealing to baby Libra as long as it's not a messy, noisy experience. After all, it's one thing to be clean and smell nice, but it's quite another to have water poured over his head and bubbles in his eyes. This little creature enjoys gentle bath-time antics – the odd duck to play with, perhaps a shampoo shield for his face – and he'll sit happily on his potty and chatter away about his imaginary world.

What baby Libra wants most from you

The ideal parent for the juggler of the zodiac is one who is fair, compromising, intellectually adept, communicative and, above all, graciously kind. But not all parents are laid-back or the fairest of them all. Baby Libra's need for constant chit-chat and the company of others might not gel with your need for privacy if you happen to be a reclusive Scorpio. She isn't interested in time-keeping because it can take too long to weigh up the pros and cons of doing one thing or another, so if you're a work-horse Capricorn with strict routines, take care.

Whatever star sign you are, it's essential that you find time to help nurture the best qualities in this baby, and define her weaknesses so she can learn to deal with those too. Explore different ideas, play with words, show her what is fair in life – and what isn't – and help her to understand that some people aren't as ideal as she'd like them to be. Baby Libra finds bad behaviour or rude language offensive, but charm, sophistication and witty company will inspire and help her to develop her own incredible debating and people-loving talents.

Teach her that too much compromise can lead to depriving herself of her rights as an individual. Help her to see that even a little confrontation isn't necessarily a bad thing. If she really means 'no' when she says 'yes', encourage her to express it

rather than fear rejection or disapproval because of what other people think of her. Explain that there is no 'wrong' answer: if something does not meet with approval it doesn't mean she's not loved. In fact your little star will eventually be the first to agree that, while love is about true balance, approval is about tipping the scales in one person's favour.

Teach her perfect manners, guide her to enjoy that rich imaginative world of hers and encourage her to make peace among her little friends. Nurture her artistic and aesthetic eye for beauty, truth and goodness. Most of all, avoid scenes, rows and arguments between family members, and teach her not to make value judgements, but to value the wonderful charm and social talents she has, and which will undoubtedly make her a star in her own right.

Scorpio

With an uncanny intuition and a probing mind, I can see right through any white lies, so remember to tell me the whole truth and nothing but!

Look at me!

With a passion for life and all its mysteries, little Scorpio is also a born spy and psychologist. Look at the way she scrutinizes your face, observes the cat, avoids all those over-friendly strangers and knows how to stay cool and mysterious when all around her is chaos. This is one sensitive, but magical, little water sign, who knows more about the mysteries of life than she lets on. From the very first day that she peers deeply into your eyes, you'll realize this is no mischief-maker. She sees right through you, and requires mutual trust and emotional bonding from the word go. It's not verbal chatter she needs, but an unspoken rapport, unbreakable and empowering. Sounds complex? Well, mysterious as she is, she can't abide secrets from others and will do anything in her power to uncover the facts. A happy baby, Scorpio is one surrounded by drama, magic and her own imagination. She will 'know' the wild wind as it whistles through the trees and she will never let you get away with excuses like, 'we can't go to the playground today because it's closed' when you're actually not in the mood. So be prepared to tell her the truth.

STAR SECRETS

Why I'm adorable
- You can't resist my hypnotic gaze
- My love is intense, deep and loyal
- I'm incredibly strong-willed and self-reliant

Why I'm impossible
- If I don't like someone I'll make faces at them
- I ask really embarrassing questions
- I have a terrible temper

My secret side
- I'm incredibly intuitive
- I thrive on intrigue, mystery and secrets
- I need a private place for indulging in my make-believe world

I like
- Loving things and hating things
- Waving magic wands
- Fairy tales, mythical characters, witches and wizards
- Playing power games

I don't like
- Being ignored
- Strangers and travelling
- People who are two-faced
- Broken promises

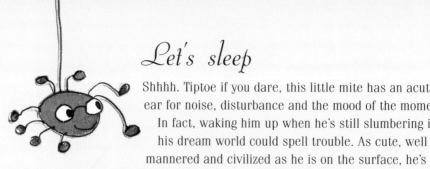

Let's sleep

Shhhh. Tiptoe if you dare, this little mite has an acute ear for noise, disturbance and the mood of the moment. In fact, waking him up when he's still slumbering in his dream world could spell trouble. As cute, well mannered and civilized as he is on the surface, he's also extremely self-willed: if he wants to sleep he will – like a log – but if he doesn't, he'll wail and howl the house down. This moody little soul will eventually find his own sleep pattern, but from the early days on expect him to nod off happily in your arms one night and demand attention the next.

Be prepared for extreme behaviour. Put a revolving night-light in his nursery and hang musical mobiles above his cot to help him sleep. Being sensitive, he'll find the dark a scary place and once he's toddling, don't be surprised if he wanders out of his nursery to tell you about the spooky things that go bump in the night. Let him know you understand and listen to his stories, even turn his night-time 'monsters' into friendly characters. They are just little friends who help look after the house when everyone is asleep and go to bed when the sun wakes up in the morning.

Let's eat

As moody about food as she is with sleep, new-born Scorpio won't slip into a feeding pattern easily. If she's hungry, she'll let you know with gusto and passion. Weaning her off the breast or bottle won't be a battle of wills, but she'll be quite clear about what she likes and what she doesn't. She has a natural instinct for certain foods, whether a large dollop of ice cream or a celery stick, and will know what's in dietary vogue!

Never assume that, because she adores mashed bananas one week, she will the next. Wisely provide a kaleidoscopic range of tastes and she'll soon let you know which find favour. By the time she's sitting at the table and holding her own spoon, her passion for eating (or not) will become more evident. Today she might simply push the plate off the table in disgust, tomorrow she'll gobble up every mouthful. Don't despair – she's only proving that she has the will to do what she wants, when she wants. Finally, be honest. If you promise to prepare some jolly jelly faces on the spur of the moment, make sure you do. Suspicious little Scorpio won't forget your promise, and she'll probably never ever forgive you if you don't keep it!

Colour and clothes

Scorpio boy

Although he's private and secretive, don't assume that dark, gloomy colour schemes will suit this mysterious character. Baby Scorpio thrives on drama, so colours like cherry red, peacock blue, luminous turquoise and avocado green should be incorporated into fabrics, curtains, toy displays and borders. His incredible imagination will be in harmony with fun creepy-crawly mobiles – themes that include friendly wizards, giants, mythical animals and magical characters from film and books.

First layettes can be either deeper tones of blue and green or snazzy stripes to add that touch of drama. Your little extremist will enjoy wearing all kinds of different styles, from bib suits to jeans and braces. He can either love a colour or hate it, and he'll soon let you know. The T-shirt with crazy cats that he loved yesterday, he refuses to wear today for no apparent reason. Bear in mind that little Scorpio likes to make his own choices as he starts toddling. Out come the shabby-chic dungarees, the Halloween cape and wizard's hat that he found in the dressing-up box. It's just the right outfit to wear when visiting (and spooking) grandma for tea!

Scorpio girl

Private little Scorpio loves to snuggle up in soft bedding, warm, rich colours and drift off to sleep watching her favourite revolving night-light or listening to her magical musical mobile. Paint the walls in soft muted tones of rose, saffron or cream, and add reinforcing deeper tones with borders, fabrics or the line up of toys on her shelf. Deep green, turquoise and midnight blue all add a touch of mystery to the atmosphere. She'll adore friendly bat, monster and witch mobiles, but make sure they're ultra friendly so she doesn't get scared.

First layettes can be brilliant white or bolder autumnal colours. She's happy in either, and this little powerhouse is always ready to move from one extreme to the other. Once she's able to make her own choices, beware. Make sure her wardrobe is full of interesting colours and textures. She adores velvety fabrics, silky scarves, hats and accessories. In winter, she'll prefer her wellies to shoes, and in summer being barefoot to wearing sandals. She'll either love or hate her clothes and anything she has decided never to wear again will be thrown furiously in the bin when you're not looking!

Let's play

Baby Scorpio thrives on mystery. Play peek-a-boo from behind his teddies,
carry him around the house investigating every object, flower, animal or
mirror as if it's a secret only he knows about. Tell him to close his eyes and
cast his spell as you wave a magic wand over his favourite soft toys and
turn them all into frogs. Wave the wand again and they're back to normal –
abracadabra! Later on, when he's toddling, play hunt the thimble, but watch
out for those probing fingers. They'll be everywhere – in light sockets, the
laundry basket, your vase of flowers and, no doubt, his first birthday cake.

This little mite will take his time when it comes to learning and developing,
so don't be frantic if he's not chattering away or crawling by the time his
little friends have already made considerable progress. Once up and about,
this is one rough-and-tumble little star, so encourage physical coordination
and plenty of activity on tricycles, toy cars, or a baby trampoline. Socially,
little Scorpio takes his time to get to know people
and will probably be most comfortable
sharing his private, magical world with just
a few very close friends. But when he does
form friendships, they'll last a lifetime.

Tantrums and crocodile tears

This baby's screams can be bloodcurdling. Early on she'll let you know with a powerful intensity from deep within her soul that she's hungry, tired or needs changing. With moods that swing further than a pendulum, baby Scorpio will resort to tantrums, breath-holding and high-pitched screams when her frustration gets to her. She'll hate to be thwarted by anything or anyone, and her need to control her world is often limited by you, family and life in general. By the terrible twos, you'll simply have to accept that she feels restricted by her own baby-ness and is less innocent than you imagine. She wants power and will get it – even if she has to howl the house down.

Botties, potties and bath time

This water baby adores bath time, so make it the event of the day. Nappy changing is a pleasure for this little one and she will kick and thrust her arms around in the air like a champion fighter. Potty training will take time and you should never be too eager. Her will-power is probably many times stronger than yours anyway: the more you push, the more she'll resist! Gentle encouragement and her growing fascination in the mysteries of her own body will be enough.

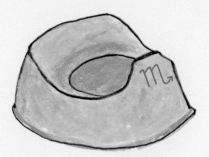

What baby Scorpio wants most from you

This complex little character thrives on absolute loyalty, truth and respect. His ideal parent is one who is emotionally sound, who knows all about life – both its fun side and its mysteries. The right kind of love for your private, and often unnervingly perceptive, star is about allowing him time to learn and develop at his own pace. Accept that he wants to wield power in a quiet, but utterly determined way. He won't want to be told off for his love-hate relationship with everything in the world. If he says he hates his favourite teddy, don't try to force him to change his mind. If he wants to plot the destruction of his tower of bricks before you get to show it off to someone, join in and scheme with him.

If you're a gregarious Gemini or extrovert Leo, remember that this tiny creature is intensely emotional and hates superficiality and frivolity with a vengeance. Your friendliness to all and everyone won't click with his suspicious attitude to new friends or chit-chatty visitors. Help him to share in the excitement of a big party of friends: set him the challenge of working out what everyone is thinking or what kind of character they have, and make it all a big mystery.

This one likes to take responsibility, even from a very young age. Among family members give this one his own share of duties or tasks, like opening your mail (ripping open envelopes is always full of surprises).

Never lie to this little creature. Never make up stories about where babies come from, or where the cat went when he died. Once he's talking, he will ask the most intimate and often embarrassing questions, so have your adult answers ready. This is one little powerhouse who can see right through deception, and his vengeance is never sweet! Baby Scorpio is passionate about life and love, so teach him that his talent for unravelling the truth is a wonderful gift. Give him total emotional honesty about your moods and feelings, and he'll soon develop his own unique talents for healing anything, from your frustration at not getting that amazing job you were after, to the cat's wounded paw. This is one star who will never let you or anyone else down if you tell him the truth.

Sagittarius

NOVEMBER 22 TO DECEMBER 21

*Cheeky, bold and hilarious, I rush around the place, chasing after rainbows
and only just have time to eat before I set off on another adventure.*

Look at me!

Your little bundle of fun is also a fiery, restless and intrepid explorer of life.
Right from day one, he'll be thrashing his legs around, gurgling, blowing
bubbles and getting up to mischief in your arms. Keeping up with him can
be the most demanding – but also inspiring – chase around the home. Quick
to walk, he'll tumble frequently, bash his toes and scrape his knees. But this
is one little star who simply bounces right back. Keep a handy supply of
plasters at the ready and pop them on with a smile and no fuss.

Baby Sagittarius likes to make plenty of noise. Early on he'll rant and rave
about anything, burble away to you all day long and ask a million questions.
And he wants answers – he has to find out 'Why?' He may frustrate you
with his madcap antics, but he's also an upfront, brave little crusader with
amazing optimism and genuine enthusiasm for life. Never pen him in, but
take him out and about as much as you can. Being stuck at
home is the last thing this spirited little creature wants.
Fresh air, strangers, travel and excitement are on his
wish list: make sure you tick them off every day!

STAR SECRETS

Why I'm adorable
- Outgoing and enthusiastic, I love meeting new people
- I'm a born optimist
- My high spirits make you happy

Why I'm impossible
- I hate being restricted by anything
- I'm a bit of a fidget and incredibly restless
- I'm always raiding the fridge

My secret side
- Freedom is my favourite word
- I want to live life to the full
- I believe in journeys, not destinations

I like
- Being a bit of a rebel
- Loads of daring or risk-taking activities
- Eating all the wrong things
- Challenges and winning

I don't like
- Playpens, prams and baby buggies
- Routines
- Being stuck indoors
- Waiting for anything or anyone

Let's sleep

When it comes to going to sleep, little Sagittarius will be unpredictable early on because she needs plenty of fresh air and activity to nod off soundly. Encourage her to stay awake as much as possible during the day. She'll adore being carried around the town in a baby sling or carrier, delighting in the passing faces, cars or countryside. The more out and about during the day, the more likely she'll find it easy to settle at night. By the time she's toddling, all that restless energy can be channelled into play and fun.

This little star will fall asleep on the floor from sheer exhaustion or doze off in the car as she gazes out of the window but, come night-time, establishing a routine will be a battle. Just let her wind down at her own pace; read exciting adventures or funny stories, play games before bedtime and let her express her zest for life throughout the day. Baby Sagittarius is quickly bored, so make her bedroom a magical place with fascinating mobiles, and giggle and laugh with her as she jumps into bed. Tell her funny nursery rhymes and explain how 'Mr Sleep' will give her a fresh batch of energy for when she wakes up to a brand new exciting day.

Let's eat

If this one wails and howls for food, he's just exercising that 'must have it now' voice at an early age. Weaning him off the breast or bottle will be easy because solids will seem such an adventure, and he'll delight in all kinds of new tastes and textures. Good-humoured and smiley, he'll gurgle away at the table if you make mealtimes exciting. The spoon might be on his head and the plate on the floor, but if you giggle and laugh at his tricks he'll bounce up and down in his seat for more!

By the time he's crawling all over the furniture his appetite will be voracious. He's a calorie burner, and a bit of a gobbler, so make sure you give him plenty of healthy, unprocessed foods. Between meals offer peanut butter on toast, eggy soldiers, fresh fruit and yogurt to boost his energy level. Living life at a frantic, exaggerated pace, means his eyes are often bigger than his belly, so slow him down by making conversation about the things you've done or are going to do that day. Teach him that talking with food in his mouth may be a laugh a minute to him, but will not impress anyone else: this little star hates to be ignored!

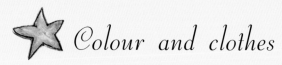# Colour and clothes

Sagittarius girl

This little mite cannot wait to be in the great outdoors, so make sure her nursery reflects the colours, light and freshness of nature. Opt for neutral shades on the walls – sandstone, sky blues and soft tones of turquoise or aquamarine. Paint a mural on one wall if you're artistic, or use adhesive borders and friezes of trees, clouds, wild animals and mountains. Keep curtain fabrics light and airy – soft muslins by day, breezy cottons by night. Appeal to her love of animals and her incredible sense of humour by hanging crazy mobiles, funny faces and a host of posters of cartoon and film characters.

First layettes can be any colour that reflect the wide open landscapes of the world. Soft greens, sea blues and earthy reds are all colours that help express her wild side. She's a bit of a tomboy, so fill her wardrobe with unisex all-in-one outfits. Include the odd frock or pinafore dress but forget the ironing: this rough-and-tumble babe would rather pull on an old pair of dirty dungarees and fall about in the sandpit than look like a Barbie doll about to go to a party.

Sagittarius boy

Mr Mischief cannot wait to get out of that cot and break free from the confines of the nursery. Make it a place of adventure and exploration in his early days. Night-lights, musical mobiles, trains, boats and planes on walls will appeal to his fascination for anything that moves. Choose from a palette of colours that reflects the great outdoors – from wild sea greens to stone, terracotta and sky blues. Complement these with fresh white and snazzy yellow fabrics and bedding. This one likes as much freedom as possible, so don't worry about baby sleeping bags or special duvets. Once he's rolling over or kicking and grabbing at rattles, he'll push off the covers anyway. This is one madcap little soul, so the more toys for him to play with when he wakes up, the better.

A clown, performer, stuntman and adventurer all rolled into one, baby Sagittarius is not one for the neat and tidy. He'll want plenty of outdoor wear once he's up and about. Choose casuals with crazy logos and a drawer full of T-shirts. Shorts, dungarees and safari gear in khaki, dirty greens and muddy browns will mean he can go out and roll around in the mud and no one will notice – at least not until you check the laundry basket!

Let's play

Bold, inquisitive and restless, this little creature is also a budding sports fanatic. Encourage physical activity from an early age and it won't be long before the explorer of the zodiac will be on the move herself. Baby gyms and swinging toys give her the chance to reach out, bat around and thrash with her legs. Wiggle hands, play pat-a-cake, bounce her on your knee. Give her the chance to feel the grass tickling her toes, go for walks on windy hillsides or make a visit to the beach so she can dip her toes in the surf and make sandcastles.

Sagittarius babies love to learn anything new, but aren't that good at finishing what they start. A painted masterpiece might end up in torn bits across the kitchen table. Instead, this one will prefer treasure hunts, playing ball and, most of all, interacting with friends and adults. Your little angel is an extrovert self-starter, who'll romp around with anyone going. She adores playing the clown and making you laugh. She often gets bored on her own, but is easily contented and will enjoy anything from a stroll in the park to showing off her unconventional amateur dramatics in front of your friends.

Tantrums and crocodile tears

This one has quite a temper. Early on, wails and screams are simply a sign that he yearns to communicate as soon as possible, but any tears will turn to smiles if you use effective diversion tactics. Baby Sagittarius really would rather laugh than cry, giggle than whimper, so be light-hearted, particularly if, at the same time, you are giving reasons why poking around in your friend's handbag is socially indiscreet. As he approaches the terrible twos the fierce, but fleeting, tantrums are just an expression of his high-energy roller-ball personality.

Botties, potties and bath time

Nappy changing can be a battle of wills: why be wrapped up like a parcel when all he wants is to feel the fresh air on his bottom? Make the experience a fun one. Chat, play peek-a-boo, laugh and make a joke of the whole performance. Talk to him as you would an adult, and tell him he won't be in these things for long. Once he's up and about, you'll probably find he's the first to throw the potty around, but he'll also be the first to sit on it. He'll adore bath time – you'll get wet and soapy, and he'll clown around in towels with howls of delight.

What baby Sagittarius wants most from you

This spirited little star, is looking for a parent who can laugh at life, but who can also show little Sagittarius how exciting the world can be. Be a teacher and a guide rather than a disciplinarian. Encourage her extrovert, often hilarious, behaviour and respect her need for space and independence. She'll adore other family members – the more the merrier – and won't love anyone particularly to the exclusion of all others.

You may not fit the model of the ideal parent, but the more you understand what makes this creature tick, the more you can try to integrate her needs with your lifestyle. For example, little Sagittarius wants to eat and throw solids around long before you (a caring Cancer, for example) have even thought about giving up breastfeeding! Later on, she'll adore messing around in the sandpit, while your partner (a Virgo, perhaps) believes she should be learning to write her name with a fountain pen. Compromise is essential with any new baby, but particularly with this free-spirited and rebellious little character. She'll adore visiting friends, stopping overnight at some unexpected location, people watching, kicking balls around and going to all

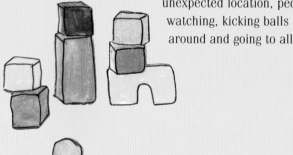

your favourite social venues. But most
of all the little clown of the zodiac wants
to be noticed, likes making others laugh and
will do anything to keep the world a happy place.

Baby Sagittarius does need to learn about
thoughtfulness. High-spirited and rebellious, she's not bothered what
others think of her and this can get her into trouble. Teach her that there
are rules to adhere to, and that learning to focus means she can also win.
Her sometimes tactless remarks can make you squirm in embarrassment.
Just remind her, without judgement, that she may think that little Thomas
has got big ears but it will hurt him to hear it from her. With gentle,
humorous discipline your little star will begin to respect that the rest of
the world will welcome her humour but not her insensitivity. As long as
you give her a long rein, she will always be in your heart. And, like the
archer she is, she will shoot her arrows out into the world, each
time with another exciting goal in sight.

Capricorn

DECEMBER 22 TO JANUARY 19

I'm quick to learn and have great table manners. My wry sense of humour has you in hoots of laughter, and most of all I want to be a grown-up like you.

Look at me!

Kind, gentle and easy-going, this little creature seems the perfect baby... but not quite. When you first gaze into her innocent eyes you'll see that, in fact, she's working you out, watching your every move and hoping that this baby business won't take too long! Little Capricorn wants to be a grown-up as quickly as possible and is often born 'mature'. This presents one little problem: right from the beginning, your little bundle prefers to do all the things adults do at the expense of the play, fun and frivolity of childhood. But her patience is phenomenal, her talents extraordinary and her serious approach to life admirable.

Offer great praise and encouragement as this little angel develops, and help her try out new things. She'll love routine and will want to master everything she does to the point of perfection. Her big heart and realistic approach to life mean she's one of the most structured and self-sufficient little souls around. 'Practice makes perfect' is her motto, but if she lets herself down she's the first to make it known. She's no crybaby, but she will feel guilty and responsible for everything – from a bird with a broken wing to why you're not smiling at your latest bank statement.

STAR SECRETS

Why I'm adorable
- Unfussy and sensible, I'm also as good as gold
- I'm loyal and will never let you down
- I have a wry sense of humour

Why I'm impossible
- I can sulk just for the sake of it
- I've got no confidence in myself
- I'm a bit of a worrier

My secret side
- I just want to be a grown-up
- I'm a serious thinker
- Discipline is my favourite word

I like
- Copying you
- Routines and more routines!
- Animals and music
- Being the best at everything

I don't like
- Going to new places
- Noisy people, letting my hair down
- Getting things wrong
- Bad manners

Let's sleep

Your little star is more like a dormouse than a goat
when it comes to sleep! He'll respond brilliantly to
specific routines, a safe, snug cot or crib and
plenty of love and affection as he dozes
off. Early on, like most babies, he'll cry
or wake when hungry or wet, but would
be much happier sleeping right through the
night. The bonus is that he'll easily get back to
sleep if you give him the right kind of comfort.
Encourage the rest of the family to share in his
routines and you'll be blessed with a very contented baby.
Make sure everyone gives him a hug or a goodnight kiss so that
you send him off to sleep with a smile on his face.

Once toddling, your baby may be so fixated with a punctual bedtime that any
change will almost certainly upset him. You might even spot him staring at
the stairs, pointing to the clock or rubbing his eyes in an attempt to remind
you it's time for him to sleep. Respect his need for order and ritual, and give
him plenty of support when he does have to change his routine. Be as
serious about his desire for structure as he is about a good night's sleep!

Let's eat

This is one little mite with a big appetite. Quietly determined to do things cautiously and in her own way, baby Capricorn needs a good feeding routine and plenty to eat. Breast- or bottle-feeding won't be a problem, although she won't want to be fussed and cooed over. 'Just give it to me straight' is her motto. Solids will be most welcome, and she'll soon have her favourite foods. Take care she doesn't get too attached to the same meals, as she isn't that interested in exploring every new purée or vegetable on offer. Gradually introduce her to other healthy meals that include some of her original favourites – mashed potato, mushy peas and chocolate in one form or another. Slow to learn, she'll watch your every move at the table: if you don't like the poached salmon your friend has prepared she won't either. Using her own utensils is great progress: praise her when she first learns to drink from a beaker alone and enjoy her determined efforts to master the spoon and plastic fork. Remember, the taskmaster of the zodiac wants to impress you and will make every effort to perfect everything, even her table manners.

Colour and clothes

Capricorn boy

'Hush, whisper who dares' will be a familiar
theme in the Capricorn nursery. Make it the
most comfortable, quiet and tranquil place on
earth. This little bundle simply wants the best
of everything, not in the glamorous way that
baby Leo does, but more in terms of quality. Bedding,
fabrics, furniture, accessories and toys must at least look
stylish and of good calibre, even if they're not. A traditional
nursery style suits this conventional little character. Use simple, classic
baby colours for the walls – powder blues, off-whites and pale yellows.
He'll adore a range of soft toys he can see from the cot as much as a
simple animal mobile and a musical night-light to help him nod off.

Keep first layettes to traditional colours, such as white or 'blue for boys'.
This one hates to be a baby, and once he's toddling you'll find him wanting
to wear what the other males in the family wear! Remember, he likes to
look good, but does not want to stand out from the crowd. Opt for classic
all-in-ones, T-shirts, shorts – even a pair of braces – in cool traditional
styles, fabrics and colours that include denim, russet browns, warm
chocolate and sensual blues.

Capricorn girl

Mature in her outlook, your baby will thrive in an equally grown-up nursery. Don't discount toys altogether, but do choose the most classical, traditional and girly styles available. Frills, trimmings, pretty toys and simple colours and textures can all be incorporated as long as they outclass those of all her little friends. Even if you have a very small budget, opt for soft white walls, lacy curtains, delicate pink fabrics and cuddly toys that complement the classic simplicity of the décor.

Serious little Capricorn will be most content wearing traditional colours for her first layette. Pink, isn't it? But she won't mind the white baby-grows and nightwear either. By the time this one is toddling, her eye for a good cut and the quality of the fabric may not be obvious to you, but she knows instinctively what looks good on her and what doesn't.

Make sure her wardrobe includes pretty little dresses, smart jackets, hats and sparkling, shiny shoes. Although she likes to be the best dressed, she doesn't like to draw attention to herself, so choose muted colours – chocolate, beige, dirty pinks, silver-greys and lavender – for her growing wardrobe of cool, spotless finery.

Let's play

Steady, slowly and at his own pace, your Capricorn star will begin to develop his motor skills. He'll adore soft toys and may have a favourite snuggle bunny, so make sure you buy a spare one for when the original gets worn out. Sing animal rhymes to him and later he'll join in quietly giggling and clapping his hands. This one is innately rhythmic. He'll respond to both music and percussive instruments, so get him banging on toy drums or even just the pots and pans with a wooden spoon.

Little Capricorn wants nothing more than to be useful. Once he's able to handle objects, encourage him to roll pastry, put fruit in bowls or unpack the shopping. Provide him with challenging, practical activities and never stop him from indulging in his make-believe world, where he pretends to be a 'grown-up' just like you. He's not the most extrovert little soul in the world, but he will thrive in adult company and will make a few special, and also very serious, young friends just like himself.

Don't push him to party, or force him to play with frivolous little angels up the road: he's shrewd enough to know not only whom he likes, but also whom he can trust.

Tantrums and crocodile tears

Business-like and efficient, this little star is happy and content if she is provided with the basic necessities of life. But beware – your baby has an effective way of showing her disapproval, doubts and fears: she sulks. Most of this stems from that friendly foe 'responsibility'. Even at a tiny age, baby Capricorn feels guilty if others are unhappy, sad or if she's not making the right impression. And she takes it personally. Rather than sob and wail, she'll pout or turn her head away, showing that she thinks something's her fault. Maybe it's because you're cross about something, or perhaps teddy has got stuck behind the sofa and no one's pulled him out. Try and encourage her to express her worries and fears, and that laughing at the world is no bad thing.

Botties, potties and bath time

Make bath time fun, with plenty of useful practical toys – scooping and pouring beakers, submersibles that send up bubbles, bobbing fish, boats and ducks. She'll adore old washing-up liquid bottles for squirting water at her toes (or you). Encourage DIY drying and putting on the pyjamas to develop her independence and cut out the complaints. She'll adapt easily to the potty, simply because she wants to be grown-up and do it herself.

What baby Capricorn wants most from you

This little mite wants a parent who is efficient, business-like, down-to-earth and on time. If you're a scatty Gemini or unpredictable Aries, this could cause the odd problem. But if you can keep to routines, set high standards for yourself and make it absolutely clear that you are as solid as a rock, he will definitely begin to trust you. Of course, no one is perfect, but the art of helping your little Capricorn to be a star in his own right is to be the kind disciplinarian, the thoughtful teacher and the responsible adult that he longs to be himself. How you feel, think, act and react will rub off on him as long as you remember his tendency to feel responsible for everything that happens. When he looks glum, refuses to communicate or seems irritable, perhaps it's you who's unconsciously sending out negative signals. If you're sure you're not, use warmth, a touch of humour and plenty of optimism to find out what's upsetting him.

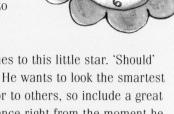

Seemingly irrelevant events can be big issues to this little star. 'Should' and 'image' are two of his favourite words. He wants to look the smartest and be the best, but often feels inferior to others, so include a great deal of praise and build his confidence right from the moment he starts to reach out for the mobile above his cot.

Baby Capricorn can make it his goal to reach the top of the mountain, but will not find it easy. Be sure to help him make the most of his innate desire for success, and encourage him to start the journey with confidence, enjoying everything he achieves along the way.

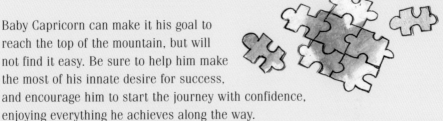

Let him grow into the resourceful, humorous and independent little star that he is by teaching him to take responsibility for his toys, friends and pets. Help develop his extraordinary learning skills with wisdom and always be there for him when he needs you. He might be a bit of an adult in baby clothing, but he is still one very insecure little soul. To loosen up those inhibitions, encourage him to sing, play music and express his feelings, and he'll reward you not only with startling honesty, but also by being the star of the smartest show on earth.

Aquarius

JANUARY 20 TO FEBRUARY 18

I'm really unpredictable and love winding you up with my cantankerous behaviour. I've a genius brain and love to be treated as an equal.

Look at me!

Put the computer out of reach and hide the television remote – your little bundle of mischief is one zany, curious person who wants to do everything in a way that is least expected of him. Defying convention – and sometimes his own limitations – little Aquarius is rather like a whirlwind blowing through your house. His 'anything to be different' behaviour means that, no matter what you expect him to say, do, think or feel, the exact opposite is more likely. Simply prepare yourself for the unpredictable. Right from the start he'll make it obvious he's a rebel with a cause: he won't sleep when you want him to, he won't eat to a pattern, and the only 'yes' you'll hear, is when it's you who's doing the agreeing. If this madcap, intelligent and smart little creature sounds like a bundle of awkwardness, that's how it is, but his original outlook on life, and his rich intelligence, will make up for all the battles of will you are likely to encounter. This one is a crusading idealist who wants to help the world and everyone in it. If you treat him like a friend and respect his outspoken, often visionary, behaviour, his wonderful talent for equality for all will shine through.

STAR SECRETS

Why I'm adorable
- I'll always be your best friend
- Creative and zany, I'm a born genius
- My unpredictable streak keeps you smiling

Why I'm impossible
- I'm a bit of a rebel
- You never know what I'm going to do next
- I love shocking people

My secret side
- I have feelings, but I don't like them
- I need to be treated like an equal
- Give me an explanation and I'll give you unconditional love

I like
- Psyching everyone out
- Being as different and awkward as I can
- Showing you how smart I am
- Fiddling with your mobile phone and computer

I don't like
- Doing what everyone else does
- Authority
- Having to sit down and eat
- Being on my own

Let's sleep

This is easier said than done. Little Aquarius has no interest in the land of nod, simply because the world is such a fascinating place. She wants to see what's going on and right from the start 'go to sleep' is not a phrase she likes. Contrary, restless and mentally alert, your bright star will not slip into a calm, convenient routine too readily. Erratic and unpredictable, her body clock is set only to the out-of-synch, mental world in which she lives. Expect sleepless nights, restless squirming and over-tiredness during the day. Once she's on the move, she'll pop downstairs every five minutes to tell you something interesting and will generally break any pattern of behaviour you try to instigate.

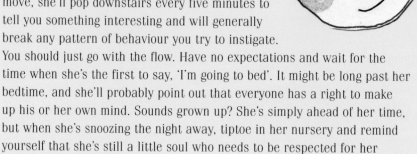

You should just go with the flow. Have no expectations and wait for the time when she's the first to say, 'I'm going to bed'. It might be long past her bedtime, and she'll probably point out that everyone has a right to make up his or her own mind. Sounds grown up? She's simply ahead of her time, but when she's snoozing the night away, tiptoe in her nursery and remind yourself that she's still a little soul who needs to be respected for her extraordinary individuality.

Let's eat

Your little genius is not always in tune with his needs. In fact, he might feed once or twice in one hour, but want nothing for the next four or five. Gradually try to establish some kind of pattern, for your own sake, without becoming a clock-watcher. Weaning won't be difficult because he'll be fascinated by the new flavours and the appearance of everything on offer. 'Ah this is something I can dip my fingers in, put on my face or pour out of the bowl upside down just to wind you up.' He's far more interested in shocking you, than gulping the puréed apple you've just lovingly prepared.

Give your little angel plenty of healthy snacks – sticks of cheese or carrot and slices of banana. Be creative in the kitchen and make creepy crawly treats, shaped like busy bees, spiders, ladybirds or mice. The weird, the whacky and the wonderful will keep him amused and encourage him to eat while you plan your next social event together. In fact, if he has a gang of little friends, go for picnics or arrange baby parties where he will instinctively share his favourite foods with everyone else. Just to be different, he might just eat everything on his plate for once!

Colour and clothes

Aquarius girl

This little character thrives on the weird and the wonderful, so make her nursery just as light, unfussy and 'cool' as she is. For walls, opt for the softest turquoises, lavenders or lilac, adding stronger, zanier colours with borders, curtains or friezes. Complement the scheme with a range of fascinating toys in bright greens, sizzling reds or spicy oranges. For bedding choose plain colours and natural fabrics, although her cot bumper can be covered in a parade of animals and funny faces.

First layettes can be bitter lemon, lavender or shell pink. This one wants to be different from everyone else, so look out for unusual colour schemes and the latest trends. Once you're out and about hunting for baby-grows, dungarees and bib suits, she'll make it quite clear what she likes and what she doesn't. In fact, you'll probably discover she's drawn to all the things you wouldn't choose for her. Once she's toddling, baby Aquarius adores proving she can dress herself better than you can. But don't be surprised when she appears with her shoes on the wrong feet, dungarees back to front and tells you this is how she's going to stay for the rest of the day.

Aquarius boy

As rebellious in his self-image as he is in his behaviour, this little mite will want to stand out in a crowd. Bright and breezy, he'll also appreciate his nursery being as different and quirky as he is. Opt for hi-tech baby toys on his shelves, fascinating mobiles and revolving night-lights to help him sleep. Keep the colour scheme neutral, but add bold splashes of colour – sunflower yellow or dramatic reds – to borders, bookshelves and furniture. Forget about bunnies and bears, your little visionary prefers trains, boats, planes, spacecraft and fantasy characters on his walls.

This little creature loves to show everyone how 'different' he is, so shock your relatives with brightly coloured layettes and the latest in baby wear. Once he's on the move, he'll need a wardrobe of rough-and-tumble-proof clothes. Look out for unusual styles and colours, patterns and accessories. He'll soon let you know which clothes he loves and which he hates. His unpredictable tastes are way-out – even incredible – to conventional friends. Anything goes with anything and the clash factor is his favourite game – more so, if it means that people stop and stare.

Let's play

A natural communicator, baby Aquarius understands very early on about language and interaction. Encourage little friends to visit and other family members to indulge in interactive play. Chuck soft balls at each other, play in the sandpit, read stories and point at things to help the little angel to understand new words. This one isn't a loner, but she is the rebel of the zodiac. In play, as in everything else, she'll be totally unpredictable. Doing exactly what she's not supposed to do is what playing is all about to her. Instead of finding your mobile phone in pieces, give her a toy phone, a toddler's radio or any of the range of baby-tech toys now available. She's a little genius in the making, remember, and once up and about, fingers will be stuck in anything that looks dangerous just to see what happens and whether she can fix or improve it.

Fill her social life with visits from friends – babies or grown-ups – the more the merrier. Head down to the local supermarket or out and about around the playground: this little star thrives on people, and that includes you. However zany, erratic and mischievous she is, remember she'll be your friend for life.

Tantrums and crocodile tears

Managing this little creature could seem the utmost test of your ingenuity and resources. He has no inhibitions when it comes to his behaviour. If his screams bother someone else, then all the more reason to shock people. This is one argumentative little star, and if his baby reasoning doesn't bring the desired result, a temper tantrum is sure to follow. Help him to develop into the original little personality he's destined to become by treating him like an equal. Eventually smiles will replace tears, and you'll get intelligent conversation instead of mixed messages.

Botties, potties and bath time

Nappy changing is rarely straightforward. This little genius really doesn't have time for all that messing about with baby powders and creams – there are far more interesting activities to think about. Early on, hang a mobile over the changing area to keep his attention elsewhere. Later, potties will hold much fascination. What can he do with it that no one else has thought of before? Instead of sitting on it, why not turn it upside down and stand on it to reach the chocolate biscuits you left on the table? Bath time is wind-up time. Be prepared for the unexpected! One day calm and serene, the next the plug pulled out or water everywhere.

What baby Aquarius wants most from you

This little mite will naturally exercise her rebellious nature against you. After all, you're a parent and, as such, her first encounter with that awesome threat to her freewheeling nature: authority. Naturally enough, for such a contrary, unpredictable person, this is just the challenge she needs to make her own personal mark on the world.

What she wants most is a parent who acts like a best friend. Guide her to accept that, although she might be unconventional, there will be limitations. If she thinks she can dress herself correctly – even if she's all caught up with arms in the legs, and jumper back to front, at least she has got the determination to try anything until she gets it right. Moreover, the ideal parent will get things wrong from time to time. This one wants to prove that she can do anything better than you can!

This pushy character loves to assert her 'rights'. Her right to say what she thinks, your right to be her friend, and also who's not right. 'Granny isn't right, it's a tabby not a tortoiseshell, I saw it in a book.' And then there's the overriding right that she can do what she wants to do, whether it is eating food off the back of the spoon or doing one thing when she said she'd do another. Be a true companion, but give her small doses of gentle discipline as well. Keep her from going off on too many tangents but don't stop her from inventing new equations about how life works.

If you're a conventionally minded Virgo, you
might feel like pulling your hair out when your
little whizz-kid causes havoc and shocks
visitors. Anything for a quiet life? Explain, explain and communicate.
Your little tornado wants more than anything to be accepted as different and
unique. If you cannot clarify why you're doing this or that, why black isn't
white and why it's dangerous to climb up on the television, she'll simply
rebel even more to prove that she knows the answer – usually in the most
unexpected and experimental way!

Cherish this unique and truly gifted little angel. Help her to develop into the
innovative, progressive individual who instinctively seeks out the new and
the different. Nurture her right to have rights, and her
underlying belief in equality for all. But don't forget,
she actually needs to know she's an equal too.

Pisces

FEBRUARY 19 TO MARCH 20

Kind-hearted and gentle, I'm the cutest soul around. There's so much love in my heart, I want to share it all with everyone.

Look at me!

Charming, sensitive and easy-going, this little creature brings a magical aura into your household, luring people into her world with sweet smiles and an innate charm. She'll twist you around her little finger in the nicest possible way just so she feels less vulnerable.

This little angel is adaptable, willing to please and gentle-natured. But too much noise, a negative atmosphere or pushy little pals will send her scuttling off to talk to her imaginary friends. Early on she'll be virtually inseparable, always wanting to be closely bonded to you. Her timidity may worry you as she clings to you for dear life, turns her face away from strangers or gazes dreamily into space from her cot. She lives predominantly in her own imagination, intuition and deepest feelings. Her moods will often emulate yours, (so keep an eye on your own behaviour and adjust accordingly). This one's charm and instinctive kindness to all things means she's the most compassionate little soul of the zodiac, crying over a dead ladybird or hugging a teddy bear with a broken paw. Her giggles, smiles and genuine empathy are extraordinary gifts, so never criticize her dreams or imagination: both are worth their weight in gold.

STAR SECRETS

Why I'm adorable
- I'll sleep through the night, and dance through the day
- I love cuddling up close to you
- I'm a great performer

Why I'm impossible
- I spend a lot of time dreaming
- Now you see me, now you don't!
- I can be incredibly lazy

My secret side
- I'm intuitive and know exactly how you feel
- I need lots of reassurance
- The fairies at the bottom of the garden are real

I like
- Going to the seaside, and feeding the ducks in the pond
- People who have vivid imaginations
- Dancing, singing and music
- Copying you

I don't like
- Loud noises
- People who are cruel to animals
- Making decisions
- Being forced to eat

Let's sleep

'To sleep, perchance to dream' should be the motto for this snuggly bundle. When he first enters the world of harsh lights, loud noises and busy people, the first thing he wants to do is go right back to sleep. In the land of nod he feels safe, calm and undisturbed. In fact you may wonder if he'll ever wake up, as he's likely to sleep right through the night from an early age. The vulnerable water baby needs big hugs, cuddles and bonding before bedtime. By day he'll need a power nap or two to restore his sensitive energy levels after being exposed to new places, people and things.

This funny creature can also be quite lazy and you might struggle getting him to wake up or out of the baby seat in the car. Establish a routine and tuck him up soundly at night, leaving night-lights on and soothing music playing before you tiptoe downstairs. The chances are he'll be eager for bedtime and, of course, his favourite fairy stories – even more so once he's up and about. The Pisces soul needs to rest after a long day's play, but most of all he loves the calm and tranquillity of his own private place – and so to bed.

Let's eat

Expect a series of lingering feeding sessions for the new-born Pisces. She will take her time, doze off mid feed and totally absorb herself in the warmth, comfort and security of your arms. This little mite may not take quickly to solids or to the adventure of sitting in her own chair. But instil a calm atmosphere, and she'll eventually get the hang of the spoon, beaker and bib, although she may require milk as a comforter long after many other babies.

This one will take her time, turn her nose up at anything that looks larger than her belly and generally get bored with the whole process of being persuaded to eat. Be relaxed, gentle and don't expect an empty plate. Baby Pisces is sensitive to food as well as her surroundings, so offer simple fare with very bland tastes to begin with. One thing you can be sure of is that her twinkling eyes and sweet smile are worth every mouthful you can get inside her. Make meals imaginative, with a touch of fantasy. After all, doesn't her favourite teddy need to eat as well? Invite him to the table, giving him his own plate and mini portion. She'll soon want to feed herself as well as him.

Colour and clothes

Pisces boy

This little angel thrives in a calm nursery. Opt for the palest of wall colours in soft blues and turquoises. The outside world is a frantic place for this gentle soul, and he'll feel secure in his cot, surrounded by images of friendly fish and animal mobiles. By the time he is toddling, he'll adore the sounds of wind chimes dangling in his window and sparkling ocean colours in the room.

Keep first layettes to blues, soft yellows and aquamarines. As he outgrows the all-in-ones, he'll take a great interest in what he wears. He's a natural actor, so what better way than to dress up and pretend to be someone else? Expect him to hate wearing his first pair of shoes. Pisces toddlers literally need to feel the ground beneath the soles of their feet to convince themselves that the earth is a reliable place. Allow him the luxury of staying barefoot whenever practically possible. He's not a rough-and-tumble boy, but he doesn't want to be dressed up like a doll either. He'll feel happier in loose-fitting, unfussy clothes with the minimum straps, zips and buttons getting in the way. Real body freedom is essential for all that dancing around.

Pisces girl

Your water baby is acutely sensitive to her surroundings, so colours, textures and decoration should be muted, soft and magical in order to harmonize with her dreamy personality. Choose subtle watercolours – dove greys, soft lavenders and gentle pinks for her nursery walls. Add magical mobiles, stars on the ceiling or fairy tale wallpapers. Soothing music can enhance the stress-free environment that she needs to feel safe and secure.

Introduce her gently to the world of fashion, choosing natural fabrics and the subtlest of colours for her first layette. White is too harsh for her, so dress her in pastels – pale blues, aquamarines and pinks – so that, as her vision develops, she can respond to the extraordinary world of colour in her own time. As she starts to toddle about, dreamy Pisces will love the most feminine clothes: pretty hats, party dresses and sweet, 'little girl' outfits will make her feel like the real-life princess she loves to hear about in stories. She adores dressing up for any occasion, whether an outing or her own imaginative playtime drama. Where did you leave your brand new evening dress? Look in the nursery and you'll see your little angel struggling in or out of it as she babbles to the raindrops on the windowpane.

Let's play

This little mite loves to mimic you. Even in the first few weeks you can make faces, play toe and finger games and chat away to keep him amused while you do the chores. He learns quickly by watching you and listening to everything you do. Notice how he gurgles and babbles away to himself, perhaps trying to emulate that nursery rhyme you sang the night before? He's in tune with the world of make believe, so fairy tales at bedtime, pretend play with favourite toys and illustrated board books will keep him amused for hours.

Even if you don't have a garden, try to get out to the countryside or a park, dig around in a flowerpot or roll on the grass with him and listen to the birds. Scrunch up leaves together and introduce him to the next-door neighbour's cat or the local ponies. Just being close to animals has a grounding effect on this highly imaginative soul, who needs to appreciate the difference between soft-toy animals and those in the big wide world. He's shy to begin with, but as his confidence grows you'll soon discover his natural talent for making other people happy. In fact, he'll eventually become the most gregarious and light-hearted little boy around.

Tantrums and crocodile tears

Your water-sign baby is influenced by the feelings of those around her as well as her own. This can often result in wails, tears and sobs for apparently no reason known to you. She is incredibly sensitive to everything, from the men drilling down the road to your moods. She'll get upset if you are, and will shriek if you're hoovering around her cot. Later, when she begins to become more sociable, it'll be your little angel that has her arm around a forlorn and lonely friend, not the other way round.

Botties, potties and bath time

Don't fuss or moan about the world while you're changing nappies, she'll just pick up on your negative vibes and associate it with misery. The potty is a curious thing. She'll be enthralled by her own achievement, but don't expect an overnight success. Remember that she likes to copy to learn. Bring in a guinea pig – an older brother, a sibling or a toddling friend! Bath time? Of course, little Pisces adores water. She'll spend hours playing in the bath with her fantasy friends, the ducks, and all kinds of water toys. Enjoy this part of the day, make it a routine before she goes to bed, and she'll be one happy little fish.

What baby Pisces wants most from you

Pisces has a deep connection to everything spiritual, imaginative, dreamy or other-worldly. Trust in his almost psychic abilities. Teach him to value his innate talent for kindness to all things, but at the same time show him how to live in the here and now without trampling on that 'other world'. Little Pisces needs a parent who understands his mystical affinity. Accept that he's a changeable, loving, healer; that he can hear the grass grow, whisper to horses and sing with the fairies at the bottom of the garden. With one foot on planet earth and the other somewhere else, he is the most loving and gentle soul you could wish to meet. The ideal parent must trust in the watery realm as much as this little angel does. All new-born human beings want to be loved for who they are, not what we as parents want them to be. This is most true for the Pisces soul, who would easily and willingly adapt to any role you chose for him just to make sure he is loved. But if he is always pretending to be something he is not, he'll be unable to set his own boundaries or know exactly who he is.

This creature wants a parent who can play make believe, who provides a safe, tranquil and low-pressure environment, who doesn't push him to perform for the sake of achievement, and who doesn't expect him to compete in the rat-race.

If you're the pragmatic, intellectual go-getter type, who believes in academic success and how many gold stars your child will get at school, then you risk misunderstanding your little Pisces. It's up to you to share his dreams, and interpret his moods.

Introduce him to the natural world, encourage him to look after the pet cat and nurture his extraordinary creative talents and imagination. The mysterious world of baby Pisces might seem as far away as planet Neptune, but that may well be where he comes from! He understands the stars and knows of places that you will never dream of (unless you're a water sign yourself). Treasure his dreams and incredible compassion, and you'll be rewarded with one star of the zodiac who can inspire and love others for who they are, not what he wants them to be. Likewise, if you show him what unconditional love is all about, funnily enough, the little copy-cat will begin to love himself for who he is too.

Index

Acknowledgements

Author
Thanks to Chelsey and Brenda for all their support, and everyone else involved in publishing this book. Also big hugs to Jess and Damien for being stars in their own right.

Executive Editor Brenda Rosen
Editor Jessica Cowie
Executive Art Editor and Designer Sally Bond
Illustrator Christiane Engel
Production Manager Louise Hall